"To women of all ages and stages of lif all know what it feels like to look to dering why our story doesn't look like reminds us instead to look up. Full of ....ugement and stories that will make you both laugh and cry, *You Are Not Behind* will be your timely reminder that God is still pen to paper writing a beautiful story for your life."

—**Morgan Krueger**, author of *Goodbye Hiding, Hello Freedom*

"Are life's circumstances writing a script that tells you God isn't trustworthy and good? If you answered yes, this book is your divine appointment. Sharing tenderly and vulnerably from her heart, my dear friend Meghan takes you on a perspective-changing journey. The practical tools and deep biblical truth she shares will both equip and encourage you to stop living according to your dreams and expectations and discover how to live according to God's good plans and purposes. They are better, my friend. So much better."

—**Wendy Blight**, Biblical Content Specialist for Proverbs 31 Ministries and author of *Rest for Your Soul*

"With the voice of a trusted companion, Meghan offers a rallying cry for those feeling stuck, trapped, and behind in life. Weaving together hard-won wisdom with the truth from Scripture, Meghan creates a tapestry of resilience and hope, encouraging us to lay our deepest aches and longings before the Lord. If you are looking for a gentle guide on your journey away from comparison and toward fullness in Christ, look no further than Meghan, as she has mined gold from her own experiences that she generously shares within these pages."

—**Audrey Elledge**, coauthor of *Liturgies for Hope* and *Liturgies for Wholeness*

"If everyone you know is moving forward with their lives while you seem to fall further behind, don't miss this book. Meghan's timely wisdom and fresh voice are what you need in a world where comparison often breeds insecurity and despair. *You Are Not Behind* assures you that you are exactly where you need to be. Let Meghan's words inspire you to reclaim your confidence, rediscover your purpose, and build a life that reflects the beauty of your unique journey with faith as your compass."

    —Jennifer Dukes Lee, author of *Growing Slow, It's All Under Control*, and *Stuff I'd Only Tell God*

you

BUILDING A LIFE YOU LOVE

are

WITHOUT HAVING

not

EVERYTHING YOU WANT

behind

meghan ryan asbury

HARVEST HOUSE PUBLISHERS
EUGENE, OREGON

All Scripture verses are taken from the Holy Bible, New International Version®, NIV®. Copyright © 1973, 1978, 1984, 2011 by Biblica, Inc.™ Used by permission of Zondervan. All rights reserved worldwide. www.zondervan.com. The "NIV" and "New International Version" are trademarks registered in the United States Patent and Trademark Office by Biblica, Inc.™

For bulk, special sales, or ministry purchases, please call 1-800-547-8979.
Email: CustomerService@hhpbooks.com

▶ This logo is a federally registered trademark of the Hawkins Children's LLC. Harvest House Publishers, Inc., is the exclusive licensee of this trademark.

Cover design by Good Mood Design Company
Interior design by Janelle Coury

You Are Not Behind

Copyright © 2024 by Meghan Ryan Asbury
Published by Harvest House Publishers
Eugene, Oregon 97408
www.harvesthousepublishers.com

ISBN 978-0-7369-8823-0 (pbk)
ISBN 978-0-7369-8824-7 (eBook)

Library of Congress Control Number: 2024931185

All rights reserved. No part of this publication may be reproduced, stored in a retrieval system, or transmitted in any form or by any means—electronic, mechanical, digital, photocopy, recording, or any other—except for brief quotations in printed reviews, without the prior permission of the publisher.

Printed in the United States of America

24 25 26 27 28 29 30 31 32 / BP / 10 9 8 7 6 5 4 3 2 1

For Brenna:

You not only lived this alongside me,
but you have lived it better than anyone I know.

TABLE OF CONTENTS

Foreword

BY LYSA TERKEURST

THE LAST TEN years of my life have included a lot of tears. Fears. Intense heartbreak. Countless hours of counseling. Wondering and asking God, "Why?" Making a tiny bit of progress. Then regress. Feeling so unsettled. Trying to step forward but wondering where to go. Secretly thinking everyone else is figuring this out but not me.

The death of my marriage left me feeling not only behind but completely devastated.

I don't know what pain you are carrying today, but chances are you have arrived here with some of these same feelings too.

You didn't think life would be like this. You didn't think circumstances would be like this. You didn't think you would be like this. You didn't think they would be like this. You didn't think God would be like this.

I have said these words. I have been in this place. I promise I understand.

But this is what I've come to know: Our life may be different than what we thought it would be, but it can still be good.

A day is coming when there will no longer be a gap between our expectations and experiences. They will be one and the same. We won't be hurt. We won't live hurt. We won't be disappointed, and we won't live disappointed. Not in people. Not in ourselves. Not in God. Our feelings and faith will nod in agreement.

But as you know, we don't live there yet. Therefore, what can we do today?

I have a challenge for you...and it's one I've gleaned from my friend Meghan many times:

Get your hopes up.

The enemy wants us to be so consumed with our unmet expectations that we lose sight of Jesus completely. He wants our inner selves to be sick with hopelessness (Proverbs 13:12), full of doubt, and disillusioned with our circumstances, other people, and God.

Oh friend, don't let the enemy get you down. Instead, get your hopes up.

You may have experienced twists and turns in your story. Distractions and delays. Undeserving interruptions and setbacks. But even when everything else seems uncertain, the goodness and kindness of God is something we can count on and something we can build our hope upon.

In the pages of this book, your tender heart will be cared for by someone who gets it. Meghan is honest and vulnerable and chooses to bravely go first—saying the things most of us feel but are too afraid to say out loud. This is not a book full of self-help hype about how to make your life better. This book is full of rich scriptural truth that will point you to the Bread of Life—Jesus. Your sustainer and Savior, the author AND finisher of your story (Hebrews 12:2).

Meghan will help you learn to live in hopeful anticipation again as you realize you are not behind. You are right where you're supposed to be. Full of potential. Full of possibilities. Full of purpose.

I know this to be true because I know Him.

Much love from me to you, friend.
—Lysa TerKeurst

How Did I Get Here?

NOVEMBER 2018

I lay on my bed and stared at another popcorn ceiling.

The ceiling started to blur as tears ran down my cheeks.

In my midtwenties, I had just moved into my eighth house in eight years, with my thirteenth roommate—wait, make that fourteenth roommate, another one had just married. I really hoped this most recent move would be the last one for a while. But there I was. Different roommate. Different popcorn ceiling. But the same feelings hovered just beneath the surface:

How did this become my life?

Did I miss something?

Am I ever going to be where I want to be?

The five-year plan I'd mentally made for my life did not include having a million roommates, moving every year, living in my hometown, being single, dumping my life savings into a hand-me-down car, and working a job I sort of hated. It featured a cute husband, maybe a kid or two, a house we owned, a golden retriever, and a white SUV with tan leather interior and a sunroof.

But right then, I silently cried at the ceiling as I wondered where God was, what he was doing, and whether anything would ever change.

Not only was I questioning how in the world I had gotten to

that point, but I also had no idea how to move forward. I felt stuck. Everything I wanted to change was out of my control. Looking back now, maybe I had more power to change things than I thought, but every single area that I wished was different seemed to hinge on something just out of my reach. I didn't get to write the script for the life I longed for. All of it seemed totally unfair.

We'll talk more about this a little later, but back when I was 21, I had decided to go all-in on the following Jesus thing. As long as I followed the rules, I assumed, God would give me the life I wanted—though I now understand this is really *not* how faith works. But as the years passed and life wasn't turning out as planned, I silently started to feel like God was holding out on me. I found myself saying: "God, if this is plan A for my life, I no longer want it."

AM I MISSING SOMETHING?

It's not that I had a bad life. In fact, on paper, some would say it was a great life. I had checked a lot of those adulting boxes: I had good friends, was young and healthy, and got to travel to cool places for work. I somehow even managed to afford to live by the beach.

But the issue wasn't what I had; it was what I didn't have.

I couldn't understand why God wasn't cosigning the life plan I had written—especially since he seemed to be doing that for everyone else I knew. That simultaneously made me question him and myself.

Have you ever felt this way? As though you got stuck with a life you never wanted? As if everyone but you seemed to have gotten the memo on how to get what you want?

Maybe you feel as if people keep graduating to new phases of life, but you're the only one not moving on from where you are. Whether you're watching another friend get married or have a baby or buy a home or get promoted, it's easy to look around and wonder: *Did I miss something?*

In those moments I often start questioning myself: *Am I not in the right city or at the right job? Did I miss what God was calling me to do? Is this a result of mistakes I've made? Why does it seem like things are happening for everyone else but me?*

Where does this tension come from?

For the first 18 years of our lives or so, many of us are on the same playing field. We go to school, we have our activities or sports, and we hang out with our friends. Then everyone goes in different directions. All of a sudden, we can be the same age as the person next to us but in a completely separate life stage. Your peer may be married with three kids in the suburbs, while the other is living in the city and climbing the corporate ladder.

And then there are people like me, wondering what on earth a 401(k) is and swiping through apps, trying to find a seemingly normal person to go on a date with.

For so long, we are taught to work toward mile-markers and goals. Go to school, get good grades, study hard, and get summers off. Maybe you go to college or get a job after graduating high school. But then what happens?

Depending on where you live and your family of origin, you can experience varying cultural pressures of what your life is supposed to look like. What's expected of you as a 28-year-old living in New York City can be vastly different from someone in Birmingham, Alabama.

We also have an ever-present reminder of what is going on in the lives of friends, family, and strangers: the rabbit hole called social media. The internet is a kind of wonderland that shows us something different from reality. It can trick us into believing everyone else's lives are better than ours.

Plus, what if we don't know what we want to do with our lives? Or who we want to be?

It's no wonder we constantly feel behind.

If we're not feeling behind, maybe we're feeling like our lives haven't started yet. Or worse, maybe we're worried life has already passed us by.

IT'S POSSIBLE TO BUILD A LIFE YOU LOVE

Though it's been years since I cried and stared at that particular popcorn ceiling, I'll confess something to you: My life still doesn't look anything like I thought it would at this point.

Many days I'm disappointed by my reality because my circumstances haven't yet been tied up in a pretty bow. Maybe you have similar circumstances you wish were different. Or maybe a gap exists between where you are and where you want to be, but you just aren't sure what you can do about it. If this is true for you, I want to invite you to go there with me, because I think we may both come out the other side a little better than we started.

Because today, I can say with full confidence that even though I don't have everything I want, I deeply love my life.

While I was busy wishing for so many things to be different, God filled my life with more joy than I could've dared to imagine possible. Not because I cracked the code to happiness or manipulated myself into delusional optimism with Band-Aid Bible verse answers. But because I realized true satisfaction can be found between where you are and where you want to be.

Maybe you're thinking, *Sounds great for you, Meghan, but that doesn't seem possible for me.* Which you have every right to think.

For a long time, I thought that way too. Which is why I'm glad you are here. You could have picked up any book today, but you chose this one. I'm not sure how or why it made its way to you. Maybe it was the intriguing title or cover. Maybe it was a gift given to you by someone who was not-so-subtly trying to tell you something.

But maybe you're simply holding this book because life doesn't look like you thought it would. Maybe you're disappointed with where you are and struggling to move forward.

True satisfaction can be found between where you are and where you want to be.

I have been asking myself one really big question, and as we take this journey together, I want to ask it of you too:

> What if we are missing the best parts of our lives because we are too busy looking around us?

I especially feel this tension when I look at the generation I'm part of and the one coming behind me. Sometimes it keeps me up at night. I'm afraid we are missing out on the best parts of life because we are stuck wishing for different ones. We think true happiness and satisfaction are found in changing our circumstances, even when we actually have the kinds of lives others only dream of having.

What if God is writing a better story for your life—a story that is unfolding right in front of you *today*? Your life is not "out there" or coming "someday," but it's happening right here, right now.

Hebrews 12:1 says God has marked a race for us to run, but we get exhausted from chasing the lives of people around us. We're running endless laps around a track trying to keep up with people who had different starting points. Plus, you may be training for the Boston Marathon when your race is only a 5K, a trail run, or heck, even a nice jog on the beach. Not to mention, we have our own junk—that is, our sin—weighing us down and making us want to numb out.

The race of life is not actually a competition. We're not stacked up against each other. You aren't losing, and the person running their race near you isn't winning. The race features runners going in different directions, at different paces, facing different hurdles along the way. But the finish line is the same: eternity with Jesus. When we take our eyes off him to focus on the racers around us, we can trip, get hurt, or throw ourselves off course.

But when we focus on what God has given us, we find a better way to live—a way to stop endlessly striving to catch up.

What if we learned to love where we live without wishing we were somewhere else?

What if we embraced our talents and found delight in the things we do for work and fun instead of looking at what everyone else is doing online?

What if we built real, authentic communities with the people in front of us instead of feeling left out?

What if we found confidence in the races God marked for us instead of trying to chase different ones?

It's possible. More than that, I think it's urgent because we have an enemy—the devil—and that enemy would love nothing more than to slow you down, sideline you, or convince you to quit. You have a part to play in building the kingdom of God, but the devil knows it's really hard for you to do your part if you're distracted and feeling behind.

When we focus on what God has given us, we find a better way to live.

DON'T MISS YOUR LIFE

Often I tell people, "I almost missed my life." God has used a series of small decisions to drastically change the plans I had for myself, which we will talk more about later. When I get caught in the trap of trying to keep up, I remind myself that I could've missed so much. And I don't want either of us to miss a thing.

I can't promise you'll never feel behind again after finishing this book. And this book won't show you how to get ahead, or help you get every single thing you want out of life.

But if you stick it out, I can promise you'll start to see your life differently.

You'll see how the place right in front of you has more to offer than you give it credit for. God has a great purpose for you, where you are, and I want to help you live it out.

Right here in the middle of the messy and mundane, something bigger is at play.

Your life matters.

Right now. Today. Not tomorrow. Not someday. Not when you get to another season or destination. And I don't want you to miss it.

So, are you ready?

Let's do this.

CHAPTER I

Will I Ever Catch Up?

OCTOBER 2019

Fast-forward several months from crying at the popcorn ceiling, and I found myself unexpectedly moving to Charlotte, North Carolina—a city I'd never visited and where I knew no one.

I had recently quit my job and wasn't 100 percent sure what my next step would be. But a few weeks after quitting, I was offered a new position that seemed like the perfect fit, the type of job I hadn't known existed until I read the description. Shortly after accepting the job, I packed up my entire life, drove for nine hours, and arrived in Charlotte on a Friday afternoon. Then I started my first day of work on Monday morning.

My worries about being behind suddenly seemed to fade away. I had gotten my dream job and left my hometown, so the possibilities of what could happen felt endless. Life started to go in the direction I had wanted it to for so long; my hopes were high.

Shortly after I settled into my new city, my friend Madi bought a house and decided to renovate it. This was *very* on-brand for her because she is always down for an adventure. She also asked me to move in, and because I love being the sidekick to my friends' dreams, I thought that sounded like a great idea. I even offered to help her with some of the house projects before I moved in.

Two twentysomething women armed with some power tools and YouTube? I'll let you imagine how that went.

One of the first projects we tackled together was taking out the popcorn ceiling in the living room. Finally! A house without a popcorn ceiling. To me, that was a sign from heaven above; ripping out the popcorn ceiling represented upward mobility.

The days of crying at an ugly, out-of-date ceiling were over. No more feeling like I was behind.

However, we were a little overambitious with our execution and basically destroyed the drywall. We had to rip out the entire ceiling and get help putting in a new one...twice. That was the end of my DIY house endeavors.

Once we replaced the ceiling, life in our little house settled down. Then about nine months after the move to Charlotte, the newness of the job and the city wore off—and I found myself, once again, staring at a popcorn-less ceiling this time, tears streaming down my face wondering why my change of circumstances hadn't changed my heart.

Wasn't this what I had wanted all along?

So many prayers had been answered. Work was going well. I'd finally found a community in a city where I hadn't known anyone. Sure, I was on roommates 16 and 17 (and *really* hoped I wouldn't make it to 20). But overall, life seemed to be moving in the direction of my hopes.

So why wasn't it enough?

THE REALITY OF STARTING OVER

Leading up to that moment, I had wrestled a lot with God. Though the move to Charlotte provided so many things I'd wanted for so long, it also revealed all the faulty beliefs I had about myself and God. What I thought was a solid foundation of faith beneath me actually had a lot of cracks. I had come to believe certain things about God based on how my life was going, which made me think I had to earn his love or make up for lost time. And I didn't know how to identify those lies, let alone know how to start fixing them.

I remember when Madi and I looked up after three straight days of scraping the ceiling, we knew something didn't look right. Instead of a smooth surface that simply needed a fresh coat of paint, we saw dented sections of peeling drywall. We Googled repair options and even called our dads to ask what we should do next.

By then, the only way to fix it was to tear the whole ceiling down.

We were so defeated. We thought we'd followed the steps. The job had seemed so simple at first, though it had taken a lot of time. Surely there had to be a way to salvage it.

But sometimes the only way to fix something is to start over.

My move to Charlotte had been a fresh start. But once I got there, I still felt like I was constantly trying to catch up. I hustled for friendships, trying to create a quick sense of home, but my efforts were exhausting.

The people I met in Charlotte were becoming dear friends, but I still didn't feel completely emotionally safe and known—not because my friends didn't create space for me, but because I was scared. For a long time, I didn't know what I was so afraid of. But as I processed my situation with some wise mentors, I realized I had *many* fears. Of rejection. Of being too much. Of needing more than friends could give.

Sometimes the only way to fix something is to start over.

On top of that, I was still the new girl. A lot of the friendships in my social group existed before my arrival. Everyone else seemed settled and comfortable, and since most of my friends were married or getting married, they didn't seem to need me in the same way I felt I needed them. They already had built-in best friends and roommates.

Even though I loved my new job and thought I was good at it, I felt like an imposter sometimes. I deeply feared that my weaknesses would eventually show, at which point I would no longer be seen as capable. Or I worried someone better than me would come along, meaning I would no longer be needed. I was working alongside really talented women who had been doing our job longer and were clearly better at it than me.

Even deeper, anxiety lurked under the surface, saying maybe God wasn't who he said he was. I knew the Bible says he is compassionate and kind (Psalm 103:8), and that he has good plans for me (Jeremiah 29:11). But in all honesty, when I looked at my own life, none of that felt true—which made me wonder if everything I had given my life to wasn't real or worthwhile.

Lots of those staring-at-the-ceiling moments have occurred when things are slow and quiet. When the rush of the transition ends and the promised other side is no longer exciting. In the stillness, I have to face what I don't want to: the loneliness, the anxiety, the fear.

Starting over strips away the stuff we love and shows what we put our security in.

Before moving, so much of my identity had been wrapped up in where I lived, who my friends were, and what I did for work. I didn't even realize how much I placed my value in them until all of those things changed.

If you've ever seen a demolition, you know it's messy. Everything is covered in dust and broken into pieces. It doesn't look like beauty can come from it.

Finished products are much more appealing. The work is already done, and all you have to do is enjoy it. I'd much rather buy a brand-new house than one I'd need to renovate—mostly because I now know I'm not good at house projects.

Starting over strips away the stuff we love and shows what we put our security in.

Madi can testify to how bad I was at remodeling. Not because I wasn't a team player or incapable of figuring it out, but because I really don't like trying things when I know I won't be good at them. I would rather pay an expert to take care of something than learn how to do it myself. Getting it right could take too long for me, or worse, maybe I could *never* do the job well enough. My oldest-child-rule-following-perfectionist self does not do well in those situations. One time I hung my own curtains, and I almost fell apart trying to get them even! To this day, I just don't look at them too closely because doing so will send me into a spiral.

We often want to fast-track and shortcut our way to where we want to be.

I wanted a new city, new friends, and a new job so I could make all my internal questions, feelings, and insecurities disappear. I had spent the early years of my twenties working on myself, and I was ready for the work to be done. Instead, I found myself more insecure and uncertain than before.

I felt exhausted. Hadn't I already been here? Wasn't I supposed to be further along?

IS IT OKAY TO NOT BE OKAY?

Soon after the crying at the ceiling incident in Madi's new house, I went back to my hometown in Florida for the holidays. There, I sat around a bonfire with my old roommates, Brenna and Shelby, along with my three younger siblings, Patrick, Abby, and Micah.

We were in the backyard of my old house, the one where Brenna and Shelby still lived. We called it the Bae House because when we all moved in together in 2016, *bae* (meaning "before anyone else") was popular slang. Plus, we lived two blocks from the bay, so the name was also a play on words. I promise we were not as uncool as that all sounds.

The Bae House originated at 54 Little Canal, when Brenna lived there with her roommates Lucy and Ebie. Then Lucy got married and Ebie moved away, so Shelby and I moved in. A year later, we got kicked out because the owners sold the place, but we ended up moving right next door to 44 Little Canal. (I'll tell you more of that story later.)

That house was the last place that had really felt like my home. The three of us clocked a lot of life together over almost three years. Brenna and Shelby were my best friends, and in a way, they became my family. In my new city with my new roommates, I had been desperately trying to duplicate that situation.

Back to the night of the bonfire. It was around my birthday, so we played a game of Meghan's Birthday Questions. I can't take credit for the invention of this game, and since we don't remember where it first originated, now anyone who knows me just calls it Meghan's Birthday Questions. The game has become a tradition in almost all my friend groups.

I always ask the same three questions:

1. What was the high of your past year?

2. What was the low of your past year?

3. What are you hoping for next year? (Note: This answer can be realistic or totally wild.)

Naturally, my friends and siblings asked me these questions as we sat around the fire on that chilly November night. When asked about my low point, I expressed that I was still struggling with insecure and anxious feelings—that I didn't feel any better now that life had settled a little more in Charlotte.

My youngest brother, Micah, was 22 at the time, and like any 22-year-old boy, he had unshakable confidence. He started sharing his "great wealth of wisdom" about being an adult with me, listing all the reasons why I shouldn't feel insecure.

I laughed and said, "But I am way more insecure now than I was at 22."

He looked shocked. "I'm sorry, did you say *more* insecure? Shouldn't you be *less* insecure as you get older?"

"No," I said. "I'm way more aware now of what I don't know, so I was much more confident when I was younger. I wish I had the boldness I did then, but I don't even recognize that girl anymore. And the uncertainty makes me way more insecure than I've ever been."

No one seemed to know how to respond. Micah walked over and gave me a hug, which was sweet, because he didn't know what else to say. Then I immediately wanted to take back my words. I had let too much out, and now my friends and siblings could see I was not okay.

Have you ever experienced this? On the outside you appear totally fine, but on the inside, you wish people would stop asking you questions so you can keep up the charade?

In that moment, I felt exposed. For the first time, I'd allowed myself to ask the question: *Am I okay?*

No was the answer. I was not.

Everyone around me seemed to be moving forward in life, while I was stuck in a cycle of perpetual disappointment.

As I reflect on that season, I now see I wasn't just trying to catch up to physical circumstances; there were spiritual and emotional ones too. Would I ever feel at home again? Or secure? Would I ever stop wrestling with God? And was God was really paying attention to me?

That night when I was in bed alone, I cried because I felt he had abandoned me.

I realized that for the past few months, I'd thought he wasn't with me anymore. There were moments previously that he seemed so close and caring—but it had been so long since I last felt him. I wondered what had happened. And if God wasn't with me, then why did any of this matter?

Then I felt like a failure as a Christian. Aren't Christians supposed to feel God and hear him? They don't seem to question or doubt him when life stops going how they want it to. But there I was, questioning everything I thought I knew about him. And I felt really let down—disappointed that what I thought would make my life better actually wasn't all it was cracked up to be.

YOU DON'T HAVE TO MANIPULATE YOUR HOPE

We often struggle to manage the tension between excitement and disappointment. On the one hand, we can downplay things to the point they will never be good enough. On the other, we can hype things up so much that almost any outcome lets us down. In an effort to manage our expectations, we do a lot of mental gymnastics.

Or we chase the high of an experience to the point of not enjoying what is right in front of us.

Think about the last time you were looking forward to

something. Maybe it was an event, a vacation, or even a first date. Then, once it was happening, did you find yourself counting down the minutes until it was over? Or dwelling on what you would do afterward? It's hard to enjoy the moment when your mind is already on the next thing.

My mom reminded me recently how I used to act when we went to Disney World as a family. Every morning when we woke up in the hotel, I would ask, "When are we going to the park?" And I couldn't sit still until we got to the park. Then, after only a little while at the park, I would start asking, "When are we going back to the hotel pool?"

You see where this is going...The cycle would continue most of the trip. (My poor parents.)

Decades later, I like to think I've grown in this area, and in a lot of ways I see progress. But I still find myself eager to get to the next thing, and once I get there, I'm either looking backward or trying to move ahead again.

In an effort to avoid pain and discomfort at all costs, I miss what's right in front of me. Good or bad.

I think the reason we struggle to sit still is less about avoiding pain, but more about being afraid of what would happen if we stop. If we aren't trying to move forward, will we get stuck? Will everyone else get ahead and leave us behind?

When God seems distant and disinterested in me, I try to take matters into my own hands, thinking it's up to me to keep my life going in the right direction.

But a few months ago, I realized how this was affecting me. Controlling my expectations and trying to avoid disappointment was no longer working.

I realized I'm constantly manipulating my own hope. I carefully try to convince myself and God that I'm in a better place than I am. Somewhere along the way I picked up the belief that if I'm truly content, then I'll get what I want.

Which, first off, is horrible theology, but we will get to that in chapter 6.

In reality, I steal happiness from today to better manage potential sadness for tomorrow.

Whether it's a new guy I'm going on dates with, a potential new opportunity at work, or something else I secretly want to work out, I put on a front that says, "It probably won't happen anyway."

Don't let them see you get too excited, or you'll be embarrassed when you have to go back and tell them later it didn't work out.

Being hopeful feels a little naïve, and I'm too mature for that.

I won't get caught off guard because I'm realistic and knew this was going to happen anyway.

Maybe you've picked up this tendency too: constantly using mental gymnastics to convince yourself, God, and everyone else that you are more okay than you are, and that the thing you long for or circumstance you want to change isn't bothering you all that much.

Deep down, you're not fine at all. In fact, you are afraid your desire for something is the reason God is withholding it from you.

Friend, I know firsthand how utterly exhausting that way of living and thinking is.

Something has to give.

In trying to keep ourselves from getting hurt or let down, we actually avoid experiencing the life right in front of us—a life that is full of really good things.

Plus, acting like we don't want something doesn't land us any less hurt in the end. And worse? We're only bracing for *potential* disappointment, not *guaranteed* disappointment. Despite my own tendency to be cynical, sometimes things actually can, and do, work out.

In trying to keep ourselves from getting hurt or let down, we actually avoid experiencing the life right in front of us.

As I think about Micah asking me why I'm more insecure now that I'm older, I can't help but notice I'm also more cynical. Jaded, even. In one short decade, I've let my circumstances tell me a story about God that is not true. The childlikeness of the early days of following Jesus has worn off. I've started living like I believe God stays at a distance and won't come closer unless I try harder to be a "good Christian." I've adopted the false belief that my actions always come with a lesson he wants me to learn. I've assumed God isn't really interested in a relationship with me—and that the only thing he wants from me is obedience.

But the truth of the gospel means none of those assumptions are true. In fact, the opposite is true: He loved me, and you, enough to send his Son, Jesus, to die for us. (If you have questions about the gospel, or if you don't yet have a relationship with Jesus, you can read the section called "How to Know Jesus Personally" on page 199.)

I'm tired of my made-up story that puts limits on God's love and purpose for me.

I want to be someone marked by hope, who has faith in God before things work out. And even when they don't turn out the way I want them to, I still want to trust God.

I want you to be marked by hope too.

Renovations are necessary for rebuilding and restoring. But renovations start with demolitions.

When I spend time in our basement, I rarely think about the work, sweat, and dust, or about the days I woke up with a stiff neck after hours spent scraping off the popcorn ceiling. No one who comes over acknowledges the corners of that ceiling that need a little touch-up paint. They never ask about the dimmer lights we installed. Even I forget what it looked like before.

Then, every once in a while, I remember.

I remember there used to be a popcorn ceiling in that room. I remember how pointless the scraping felt the moment we realized we had to tear it out. And when we failed to install new drywall ourselves and had to rip it out again. And how Madi's dad came to help.

Renovations are necessary for rebuilding and restoring. But renovations start with demolitions.

Regardless of the time and effort invested, we eventually had a new ceiling.

So, I'm going to try a little experiment: Instead of trying to act like I'm not hopeful, I think I'm going to try to just be excited?

Is that idea as silly as it sounds? To me, it's a little scary. I haven't exactly handled disappointment well in the past. And sometimes I wonder if the next time I feel like God let me down if I'll be able to recover.

But maybe it doesn't have to be that way.

The reality is, we still have hope whether we want to admit it or not. It's how we decide to express that hope that shows what we believe.

> Now faith is confidence in what we hope for and assurance about what we do not see (Hebrews 11:1).

Hope is something hardwired in us by God.

To be joyful in hope (Romans 12:12), that hoping in him renews our strength (Isaiah 40:31) and in hoping we won't be put to shame (Romans 5:5). While my past hurts and heartbreaks make me want to protect myself, I know I'll miss so much if I don't let myself feel hopeful. Furthermore, the world is messed up enough—so why not try to enjoy the days when we can actually feel happy?

Hope is something hardwired in us by God.

We spend a lot of time robbing ourselves of the joy of looking forward to something. Personally, I've decided I'm done with that.

What about you? Are you as tired as I am of living this way?

Even as I write this chapter, I'm really excited about some things on the horizon. And I'm scared to even admit that. There's always a chance they could all go horribly wrong, and I could regret ever writing this part of the book.

But something tells me hope is worth a shot. That on the other side of living and thinking this way, I'll find even more of God and the abundant life he wants to offer me.

I wonder what would it look like to actually live a year where I wasn't trying to manipulate my hopes?

Would anything about my life look different? Would I feel any better?

Would I actually get to experience the good gifts God has tucked into each day?

Would days of happiness outnumber days of disappointment?

Would I learn to love the life I have instead of wishing for another one?

Can I get my hopes up?

To be honest, hope rarely feels like enough.

But there is only one way to find out, and as we walk through this journey together, I'll do my best to try.

Maybe we can start there: looking at the parts of our lives that need a little rebuilding and restoring. Acknowledging the moments when we struggle to believe God is with us. Admitting we are not okay.

While the process of learning to not manipulate our hope can feel messy, I think that process helps us lay groundwork for some really good things. It may take a few attempts, but like ripping out the popcorn ceiling, this step may be the start of a good story someday.

CHAPTER 2

I Feel Like I'm Missing Out...
Because I Kind of Am

I MEET THREE friends every Friday morning for coffee: Riley, Katie, and Elizabeth.

We all met through Riley, the best connector of people. Everyone wants to be friends with her because she's genuinely the easiest kind of person to be around. Riley and I worked together when I first moved to Charlotte, and then we became neighbors.

Katie, Elizabeth, and I moved here around the same time. Katie and I had mutual friends, and she is hands down *the* funniest person I know. You want her at every party because her presence guarantees a memorable story. It's hard to find someone who can bring the fun like that *and* be one of the most intentional friends you have.

Elizabeth moved from New York City, and I immediately wanted her to be my friend because she asked good questions. I also thought it was cool that she led worship. I just felt like we understood each other. She's the kind of friend who you can go grocery shopping with and leave feeling closer than when you started.

The second time we all hung out, we just decided right then and there to start meeting weekly. And somehow, years later, we've stuck with it.

We usually meet at Summit Coffee in South Charlotte because it's cute inside and is the most central location for all four of us.

The baristas know us because we always sit in the left corner booth. When we started meeting there, Katie had her son, Hayes, in tow until he started to walk. But shortly after that, she had her second child, Gracie, and she got to join our little girl gang.

We've celebrated weddings and babies, promotions and buying first homes together. They've heard the details of every date I've been on and read the roughest drafts of this book. We've even gone on vacations together. Their husbands treat me like a sister, and their kids will call me Aunt Mae Mae (when they actually start talking, that is).

These are the friendships I prayed for when I moved here. It feels rare and hard-fought for, but they are like my family.

Typically, we catch up about our weeks and sometimes vent about work. Depending on what's going on, there's a lot to share. Other times we talk about a passage of Scripture or a book we are reading together. We confess sins, pray for one another, and make space for everyone to be heard. It's one of my favorite times of the week.

I have a very vivid memory from about six months before we all started turning 30. The day is seared into my mind because I had a *little* bit of a freak-out (and by *little*, I hope you read: *full-blown internal panic attack*).

It had been a few weeks since we'd met, and a lot had happened. Katie had just given birth to Hayes, so we went to her house to meet him for the first time. Elizabeth and Grant had just gotten back from their honeymoon, and Riley shared with us how she was thinking about starting her own graphic design business. While I held Katie's beautiful new baby and listened to all this news I was genuinely thrilled to hear, I felt myself getting overwhelmed.

I had *nothing* new to share.

Not one thing. Nothing noteworthy had happened in the weeks since we had seen each other. I didn't even have the prospect of a husband, baby, or promotion. All I could think about was the milestone birthday that was fast approaching and how we would be starting a new decade in *very* different places.

Two words looped in my head: *I'm behind.*

I felt paralyzed because I couldn't fix my situation. It was just my reality. The biggest thing that had happened to me that week was getting a good parking spot at Trader Joe's. We were physically sitting in the same room, but I couldn't feel any farther away from them than I did in that moment. Even more than feeling behind, I worried I was going to get *left* behind—and I'd never be able to catch up.

The thought made me feel both sad and scared. Sad because they all were living things I desperately wanted and was unsure if I would ever get. Scared because if they kept moving forward, would they leave me behind?

Would I stop being invited to things? Would they find other friends who were in more similar seasons to them? Would I be left out because I couldn't relate?

Nothing they said or did gave me any reason to question if they would "move on" without me. In fact, as they read this, they are probably surprised I felt that way at all. But something about what I lacked circumstantially made me feel less valuable as a friend.

I wasn't a wife, mom, or business owner, so I couldn't speak into those areas of their lives with any authority or experience. While they traded stories about marriage or home ownership, I felt myself shrinking back and getting anxious.

I was so behind.

WHAT MAKES US FEEL BEHIND

What makes you feel behind?

Is it your relationship status?

Where you are in your career?

The amount of money you have, the things you own, or the place you live?

Or is it something less visible?

Is it how insecure you feel? Despite your age, do you still find yourself walking into a room and feeling small or left out?

Is it a lack of confidence in who you are? Even if you can fake it on the outside, do you worry you'll never be good enough?

Or is it another struggle you've yet to outgrow? No matter how many times you've tried, you just can't seem to overcome that same cycle you've been in for years—and you're starting to wonder if you ever will.

Maybe it's your relationship with the Lord. Do you still have questions and doubts? Do you feel like this whole Christian thing should be easier? Does everyone around you seem to have a handbook on how to get close to God, but you somehow missed that class in Sunday school?

When everyone around us seems to have it all together, we can feel like we are falling apart in comparison.

Depending on the day, any one of these scenarios can make me feel left behind. I wrestle with comparing myself to everyone else my age. Sometimes I even do this with younger people because they seemed to have figured it out long before I did. Whether I'm observing my actual friends or the people I follow on social media, it's hard not to stack my life against theirs.

Most days I am baffled by how everyone else seems to easily manage their everyday responsibilities *and* plan ahead! Because, quite frankly, I am tired, and their lives feel like a lot to keep up with.

When everyone around us seems to have it all together, we can feel like we are falling apart in comparison.

YOU ARE NOT BEHIND

Many of us feel this way—as if *others'* lives are neat and tidy, and ours is the only mess. It's easy to look at what someone else has and want it for ourselves.

Even the people who have what we want feel this way.

The married person misses the freedom of their single days.

The parent craves just one night of sleep or alone time with their spouse.

The friend crushing her job wishes she could turn off the responsibility and have more flexibility.

The messy parts of our lives make us aware of the tidy-looking parts of everyone else's.

Life just *seems* so much easier for them. And you start to fear you are missing out.

ARE WE MISSING OUT?

Phrases like *singleness season* really bother me, especially because *season* feels like a nice way to describe that. The questions that often linger in the back of my mind are: *What if this is not a season? What if this is just my life? Who are you, sir or madam, to know that for sure?!* (I am much sassier about this in my mind than I'd ever let myself be out loud.)

While I don't know the answers to those questions for you personally, I know the underlying uneasiness that comes with not knowing. And it's not fun at all.

I genuinely liked being single in my twenties. I know that's not true for everyone, and I certainly had my days. For whatever reason, my marital status wasn't the main area where I questioned whether God would come through for me; and I don't really know where that assurance came from because I questioned God in basically every other area of life. Honestly, part of my contentment was probably because I never imagined it would last until I turned 30.

But the closer I got to that day, the more my singleness made me feel behind. And as the number of friends I had getting married increased, my contentment with my situation decreased.

They all had built-in plans on Friday nights and someone to travel with and take to weddings. The days of "just the girls" were seemingly over.

The number of times the bill would arrive at dinner and it was time to split and everyone else had someone pair off with besides me always made me want to crawl out of my skin.

In a sense, I *was* missing out. I didn't have what they had.

If you're single and wish you weren't, your desire for a relationship may stem from loneliness. Or maybe you're like me, and you get tired of having to make decisions and navigate life as an adult alone. Either way, singleness can feel so very out of your control.

And as I got older, it became harder for me to reconcile that my other dreams—having kids, owning a home, and having certain types of respect and stability—all seemed to hinge on having a husband.

While there are definitely ways to accomplish those other dreams outside of getting married, they sure seemed a lot more achievable alongside someone else.

How do we move forward and act when our hopes and dreams are attached to outcomes beyond our control?

Collectively, we all have faced this reality before. After 2020, the whole world feels a little behind. COVID-19 and the pandemic lockdowns halted life as we knew it. No one could move forward. Plans were paused, changed, and canceled. Familiar routines and habits ceased to exist.

We couldn't pursue our dreams because we were literally confined to our homes.

Dating was close to impossible, kids missed school, friends didn't gather. Even churches were closed. Jobs were lost. Loved ones passed away. Symptoms lingered. Weddings were rescheduled. Marriages ended.

Normal was no longer an option. Rather than trying to keep up or get ahead, we focused on surviving the unknown. Even years later, many are still feeling the effects of the pandemic:

- Millions of people lost their jobs, and unemployment rates reached the highest they had been since the 1930s.[1]
- One in four people had difficulty covering their basic living expenses, such as food, housing, and medical care.[2]
- In 2022, just two years after the pandemic began, the expected number of couples getting married went up 15 percent to make up for postponements from COVID.[3]
- Over 60 percent of singles say dating got more challenging during the pandemic.[4]
- One in ten adults have experienced "high levels of psychological distress" since the start of the pandemic, the most likely affected being between 18 and 29 years old.[5]

And since the world has regained some sense of normalcy, doesn't it feel like we are moving at breakneck speed to catch back up? We had to slow down for a couple of years, but now the world seems to be pushing us to move faster, do more. It's almost as if we are trying to make up for lost time.

It's exhausting.

Whether it's because of the pandemic or not, we have to acknowledge the grief that comes from feeling your life is on hold. Grief doesn't just happen when someone dies. We grieve when life doesn't look the way we thought it would. Whether a dream or a relationship disappears, or a disappointment or a disaster happens, we have to deal with the grief attached to it.

Even the grieving process can make us feel behind. As time passes, we may wonder why we are not over what we have lost—as if we should be further along in the process than we are. The grief appears never-ending. Or if we finally make progress but something happens that triggers us, we can feel like we are moving backward.

We have to grieve what happened—or what *didn't* happen—in order to move forward. In chapter 5, we'll talk about how to do that. But in the meantime, how do we move forward when we are stuck feeling behind?

> ## Grief doesn't just happen when someone dies. We grieve when life doesn't look the way we thought it would.

WHAT HAPPENS WHEN WE GET HONEST WITH GOD

After I left Katie's house that day, I had a rare moment of taking some ownership over my life. Instead of sitting in the feeling of behind-ness, I decided to make a list of things I hoped to accomplish before I turned 30.

Some really ambitious people make a "30 before 30" list. However, I was a little late to this party, so I only picked five things. A couple of them were goals I could work toward, but the others were a little out of my reach and control. I guess you could say my list was more a list of prayers. I wrote them down and asked God, if possible, for them to happen within the next year.

Here's the list:

1. Get a book contract

2. Start dating the guy I would marry

3. Pay off the remainder of my student loans

4. Beat my high school running time for a 5k

5. Read 30 new books

I feel vulnerable sharing these with you. I felt even more vulnerable asking God for them. Not because I didn't believe he could accomplish them, but because I was genuinely afraid of what would happen if he didn't.

Putting the deepest desires of my heart down on paper, knowing the slim chances of them actually happening, seemed silly. Naïve, even.

After 29 years, I had been let down one too many times before. Every time another disappointment hit, I grew more skeptical of who the Bible claims God to be. Of who I had previously felt sure I knew him to be.

But we can't let disappointment dictate how we define God.

Only one of those five things happened. One. If you are reading this book, you know which one it is. And don't get me wrong; getting a book contract before 30 is a *huge* accomplishment. I still can't believe it happened.

But the remaining four on the list? Three of them were sort of within my control. I could have made different financial decisions or trained harder at running. As an avid reader, I would normally be able to read 30 books with ease—but I didn't even manage that, which made me feel like a complete failure. The absence of #2— dating the guy I would marry—was also deeply felt.

When the decade changed, I had a choice to make: Did I still believe God's plan for my life was good? Or did I think he was just stringing me along?

And if I thought he was stringing me along, what would that mean for my relationship with him going forward?

Sometimes it can feel like God is dangling carrots in front of me so I don't quit on him, when he really has no intention of giving me what I want.

Then, when things look like they are finally falling into place, the rug gets pulled out from under me. The disappointment isn't really about the things I want not working out; it's in feeling like God is letting me down again. Just another instance of getting my hopes up, only for them to crash and burn.

Years into this wrong way of thinking, I discovered I've believed a lot of things about God that are just not true. In my head, I know who he is—but in my heart, I don't believe it because I've let my circumstances control what I think about his character.

As I've begun to untangle my thoughts, I think it's really kind of God to invite me into this journey of not manipulating my own hope. He's showing me that being honest with him is actually the best way to be. Not just because there I get to experience more hope, but because there I find out who he really is, which is faithful (2 Thessalonians 3:3), good (Nahum 1:7), and kind (Romans 11:22).

Can I extend that same invitation to you? Would you let yourself be hopeful, expecting to learn more about who God really is?

NAMING WHAT IS MAKING US FEEL BEHIND

Before we wrap up this chapter, let's name right now what is making us feel behind.

Whatever comes to your mind, I want you to write it down. It can be one big thing or multiple things. Something happens when we name our burdens and griefs. When we get honest with ourselves and God about what we hope to be different, we can start to untangle the lies we believe about him and move toward hope again.

Can we take a moment of honesty with God together? The grief process can feel dark. The lies we believe about ourselves and God can rob our hearts and minds of seeing what is true. So let's bring what we feel into the light.

Be honest about where you're trying to manipulate hope.

Be honest about what you want.

Be honest about your disappointment with God.

I feel behind because _____

_____.

God cares about what you wrote on those lines. He is not trying to lead you on in this process. He is not withholding good things from you. He is not holding you back from where you long to be because he is cruel. He is kind and knows what is best for you.

This is how we walk forward. An object in motion is so much easier to steer than one that is still. Even if we are moving apprehensively, it's easier for God to point us to where we are going when we are willing to take a few steps towards him.

The lies we believe about ourselves and God can rob our hearts and minds of seeing what is true.

CHAPTER 3

Wait, I'm Not the Only One?

In late August, I sat on the beach in Cape Cod, Massachusetts, with a few friends from college. The temperature was perfect for a New England summer: cool enough to not be sweaty, but hot enough to get that warm tingle on my skin from the sun. Everywhere I looked, the hydrangeas bloomed like weeds.

My friends Randi, Kelsey, Caroline, and I hadn't been together in a couple of years, and this reunion felt like a dream. There is something about being with old friends. When you have history with people, spending time with them just feels different. You don't have to explain yourself. They know you. Like *really* know you. They were there for the bad ex-boyfriends and remember all the weird phases you went through in college. Something about being fully understood brings a lot of comfort.

We chatted nonstop the whole hour-and-a-half drive from the airport to the coast, and we kept talking over buttery lobster rolls and fries at the Squire, a local restaurant and bar known for their seafood. (The lobster rolls were so delicious we went back and got them again before we left.) Every year since we graduated from college, we have tried to get together for a long weekend reunion. When I lived at the beach, they usually all came to be with me. But we had missed the previous two years—the first one because I'd moved unexpectedly, the second year because of the pandemic.

A lot had changed since we were last together. We all had new jobs, and I'd moved to Charlotte. Randi had gotten married and was living in Boston while her husband got his PhD at Harvard. Kelsey and I navigated roommate dynamics and had gone on some really bad dates, so now we laughed as we traded stories. Caroline and her boyfriend were getting ready to move across the country to San Diego. And one of them had recently lost her dad.

Yet as we hauled our backpack beach chairs, towels, and coolers down to the sand, it was as if no time had passed. We cracked open seltzers and dipped our toes in the freezing Atlantic Ocean. Caroline picked a playlist, and Kelsey started to read. At one point I dozed off and took a nap.

As the sun started to go down, we started talking about ideas for this book. My friends knew I'd felt called to pursue having a book published since our senior year, and the time had finally come for me to take some steps. I just wasn't confident of what to write about yet. And as good friends do, they started to brainstorm some ideas with me.

At one point Caroline mentioned something I had posted on Instagram that said, "You are not behind." Kelsey and Randi immediately chimed in and enthusiastically told me that they had related to it as well. I was sort of shocked and thought, *Wait, I'm not the only one?*

We were all in very different places: married, in a serious relationship, dating, and single. Making career moves and wondering if we really wanted to pursue what we were doing. Living in the Northeast, West Coast, and the South.

Yet we all felt the exact same way: *behind*. I personally related to so much of what they said, nodding along in full agreement. Maybe this was something we all struggled with.

So I asked them: What is the solution? What does the person who feels behind need? And is that enough for a book?

Honestly, none of us really had an answer. But after that

conversation, I couldn't let the idea go. For the next several months I wondered how many of us feel this way. The more I asked people I knew, and the more I posted on social media about it, the more I saw people relating to this concern in at least one area of their lives.

Maybe my friends were on to something.

WHAT WE TURN TO WHEN WE FEEL BEHIND

We all have an ache in us for more—a discontentment with life not turning out the way we thought it would. When we have moments, days, or even years of waiting for it to be "our turn," that discontentment can start to wear on us.

In the middle of the waiting, we can start to believe we are the only ones who feel this way.

When that happens, we usually try to take control of our circumstances—sometimes not in a good way.

When people get stuck feeling behind, they try to cope. Coping mechanisms can help us get through challenging emotions and circumstances, but they can easily go too far when they become the source of our satisfaction, an escape from reality, or the only way we can function.

We all have ways we overcompensate for feeling behind. Some coping mechanisms include:

- Collecting experiences (especially ones that look really good on social media)
- Overindulging and spending more money than you have on clothes, food, and trips
- Jam-packing your daily schedule because you're afraid of what might happen when you get still and quiet
- Avoiding your own feelings by staying busy and over-committing to activities

- Choosing to separate yourself from certain people or situations that might remind you you're not where you
  want to be

Or in my case, making my "5 before 30" list.

As I mentioned, some coping habits can be helpful for a period of time. My friend Victoria makes a "winter fun calendar" every year to get through the cold, hard months when it gets dark early. I've even adopted it with her because it does help me enjoy that time of year more.

The problem is these coping mechanisms rarely fix what's going on beneath the surface.

Take travel, for example. Now, this may offend some people... but traveling is not a personality trait. There, I said it. (If you are a little offended, I love you. Please still be my friend!)

Don't get me wrong; I love traveling! Getting to see different parts of the world and experience new cultures is a gift and priv-ilege. If you have the means and opportunities to go places, take advantage of them. I'm by no means saying that traveling is bad.

But when our happiness depends on whether we can go on trips, we have a serious problem. When it turns into our whole personality or part of our identity, that's an issue worth address-ing. As with any coping mechanism, we should look at what we are avoiding or running from.

Planning a trip can turn into an escape tactic. You put some-thing on the calendar to keep you going. In my life, it looks like a lot like this:

It's the dead of winter. Mild seasonal depression sets in, and I need something to look forward to. I start scrolling through social media. An influencer I follow is in Mexico. *Ugh!* It looks so warm there. I google flights. Why is everything so expensive?! Maybe I just need to go somewhere drivable instead. Within an hour, I've made plans for a couple months away.

Temporary relief comes but doesn't last. Soon I'm saving ideas for restaurants and places to visit at my chosen destination. Then I need some new outfits for the trip. Before I know it, I've got seven tabs open on my computer and I'm toggling between online shopping carts. When the week of the trip finally arrives, I can hardly focus on work because I'm ready to be on vacation!

The trip is so fun, but soon it's over. And the trip hangover is real. After every vacation, I eventually have to come back to reality—to the same feelings I've tried to avoid. To a very full email inbox. To a sudden margin in my calendar. To the nagging thought: *What do I have to look forward to now?*

I won't speak for you, but I tend to want to rush past those feelings. Does *anyone* want to face the hard emotions or do the hard work of addressing why we want to escape? Give me quick fixes and practical steps to get me to the other side as painlessly as possible.

But I think there's an invitation here we are ignoring: to find purpose in the process instead of rushing to get to the other side.

Find purpose in the process instead of rushing to get to the other side.

THE (NOT-SO-GREAT) WAYS WE TRY TO COPE

By the time I go on a trip, I'm usually crawling into it burned-out and weary from the busyness of life. In fact, before my most recent vacation, I found myself questioning things about God that I once thought I was sure of. Old disappointments showed up in new ways and hurt more than they did before. So vacation was a welcomed break. A sigh of relief. In a lot of ways, a distraction.

In some seasons of life, though, going somewhere is just not feasible. I mean, remember 2020? We could barely travel to our mailboxes!

That period of time may have exposed something in all of us. It showed each of us the many places and escapes we had used until that point to look for satisfaction and try to avoid any seemingly unpleasant emotions. It had become so easy to distract ourselves with experiences that made us feel better. We could numb any pain with a quick, temporary fix and keep moving. We almost never had to slow down and face anything head-on.

Before the pandemic, when the world was wide-open to us, anything seemed possible. Whether we acknowledged it, we felt free to go wherever we longed to go, do whatever we desired to do, and be whoever we wanted to be.

But when the lockdowns started, this was no longer the case. New limits were placed upon us. We couldn't run away every time we wanted to escape.

So instead, we turned to some more obviously unhealthy coping mechanisms. For example:

- A 41 percent increase in "heavy drinking days" has been noted in women alone since the beginning of the pandemic.[1]

- According to a survey of adults in the United States, "Excessive drinking (such as binge drinking) increased by 21 percent during the COVID-19 pandemic."[2]

- The average amount of time spent staring at screens skyrocketed.[3]

- Regular pornography consumption went up 25 percent during onset of the pandemic.[4]

On top of all of that, many studies showed an increase in struggles with depression and anxiety.[5] Because what was beneath the surface felt too painful to face. However, if we don't address what we are trying to avoid, we will never experience the abundance God has in store for us.

> ## If we don't address what we are trying to avoid, we will never experience the abundance God has in store for us.

THE CHOICE: ACCEPT OR AIM

When life stops going our way, we usually respond in one of two ways: Let's call them *acceptance* and *aiming*.

Both reactions have healthy and unhealthy sides to them.

Acceptance can look drastically different depending on your attitude and perspective. On the one hand, acceptance is looking for the good in your reality and choosing to embrace it. Usually, a person in a healthy state of acceptance is doing their best to trust God and still have hope toward their heart's desire—even if God has to change their heart first.

On the other hand, acceptance can look like sulking in your circumstances. You can easily become a victim, complaining every day until you (and everyone around you) grows miserable. This unhealthy version of acceptance has little hope.

Aiming can also vary from person to person. Unhealthy aiming looks like trying to claw your way toward the life you want. You are so fixated on the one thing you don't have that you do everything possible to get it, no matter how much it costs you.

When that doesn't work, you begin the never-ending chase for the next high—a trip to Europe, a new shirt, or another latte from your favorite coffee shop. (I'm guilty of this too!) You run from experience to experience, hoping the next thing will make you content with your life. And it never does.

However, healthy aiming can look like making lemonade out of your lemons. You focus on making the most of where you are and setting your gaze on God.

I've often heard people speak of "playing the cards you've been dealt." But I don't care for that phrase. I get it, but I don't like it. I don't see God as a blackjack dealer, you know? He's not up there shuffling cards, dealing them haphazardly, and leaving us to figure out how to win. The dealer is not invested in the outcome or helping the players win, so that metaphor doesn't sound like God to me.

But I do think God is like a gardener, as Jesus talks about in John 15—intentionally growing good things and giving us the ingredients we need to make something beautiful out of them. He takes care of what he is growing, knowing the garden is worth the time and effort he puts into it.

We often reject the very ingredients he has given us. Instead, what if we used them and made them into something?

CAN WE CREATE THE CIRCUMSTANCES WE WANT?

Learning to love my life in Charlotte was challenging, and the effort exhausted me. A friend prompted me to make a list of things I liked about my hometown that were missing in Charlotte, with the goal of seeing if I could maybe recreate some of those qualities in my new home. The step was small, but her question made me consider what I could realistically do to create some of the circumstances I wanted. So I made a list of what was missing:

1. The beach (obviously not something I could bring to Charlotte)

2. My family (again, couldn't really change this)

3. My friends

4. Living somewhere walkable to friends

5. Short commute to work

6. Not many places to spend money close by

7. Running into people I know at the grocery store

8. A slow pace of living—not having to rush from one thing to the next every day

Okay, so the first half of the list…not easy to recreate. But the second half? Maybe I could make some lemonade out of lemons there!

Let's start with friends. I needed to make good friends, which isn't as easy as it sounds. But I straight-up hustled for friends. When I came back to Charlotte after quarantining for three months in Florida, I started asking people to hang out literally every day. Sometimes even twice a day. I'd take a walk with someone before work, then have someone else over for dinner. I'd meet up at a park if they wanted to social distance, or we'd grab a drink after work and sit outside. Everyone I met with whom I thought I could build a friendship, I texted and tried to hang out with. And if it went well, I kept asking them to do stuff.

It would have been easier to wait for everyone else to initiate. I mean, I was the new girl; shouldn't they have been asking *me* to hang out? (And yes, several gals made the effort and invited me to do things.) But I knew all too well that if I waited around, I could be waiting forever—and I badly needed people who knew me and could be there for me. I couldn't sustain a life that far from home without deeply rooted friendships. And I knew those took time, so I was not wasting any.

After a while, I realized I had cast a really wide net and needed to narrow it down. I am fairly extroverted, but I also need alone time and was running on empty trying to grow some of these friendships. I picked a handful of girls I thought could become close friends and invested my time in them. (You'll get to know all of them in this book!) Part of the reason those relationships worked is because these girls also put in effort. Meanwhile, some of my other friendships took different shapes. Maybe I didn't see those people weekly, but we still made enough time for each other to be close. Other acquaintances eventually fell off.

And that's how I made friends. This was the most time-consuming item on my list.

At the time I made the list, I was living closer to Uptown Charlotte and really loved being so close to all the excitement of the city. As a newcomer, I got to experience the "city girl life" my small-town self had dreamed about. I had great roommates, could walk to my favorite park in town, and was close to fun restaurants and things to do.

But my excitement eventually wore off, and I craved the feeling of something more intimate—as you can see from the latter items on my list.

Then Madi bought her house. It was significantly closer to my work, a little farther from the hustle and bustle of the city, and in a neighborhood where two good friends already lived. I had not planned on moving, but I felt like God was handing me something that would help me make Charlotte home for a longer time.

A shorter commute meant a slower pace and less rushing from activity to activity. Sure, life was busy and my calendar was still full, but it felt more manageable. And I can still remember the first few times I ran into people I knew at the grocery store. I felt like I really lived there. Charlotte started to feel like home.

It did require effort. But I didn't have to do it all on my own.

DOES ANYONE ELSE STRUGGLE WITH HOMESICKNESS?

At some level, maybe we all long for home.

We want a safe place to run to when life feels too hard. Or a memory we wish we could bottle up and keep with us forever. We may not long for a physical place, but rather a feeling. The feeling of being secure, innocent, light, and free.

I think under the surface, I'm always a little homesick.

When I moved to North Carolina, I had to let go of the place I'd called home my whole life. Sure, it would always be there to visit; my family hasn't gone anywhere. But that *feeling*. I miss that feeling. And while my old hometown no longer feels like home, where I am now doesn't totally feel like home either.

Something about that makes me feel behind. And I wonder if I'll ever feel "caught up" if I don't own a house or have a more permanent roommate.

Maybe it's because I've moved a lot and had a gazillion roommates, but along the way I decided that "making a home" as quickly as possible whenever I moved mattered a lot to me. Since I don't always know how long I'm going to live somewhere, I try to unpack as fast as I can—put pictures in frames, hang the curtains (even if I still get extremely flustered when they are uneven), and invite people over.

I've managed to build a home in a lot of places, turn roommates into family, and create memories that will outlast the address on the mailbox.

And yet, when those things come to an end, I can get really, *really* sad. You've already met some of the faces and places I've come to call home, and constantly having to move has created this ache in my heart for stability. I long to feel like I'm not going somewhere else—like I'm where I'm supposed to be.

Madi's house has become more of a home than I dreamed. She, Ali, and I have made a lot of memories there. We've formed a family in that neighborhood (something we will talk more about in a couple chapters).

But this phase will have an end date too. Though we have put so much work into her house together, and she has genuinely opened it up to me, the house still belongs to her.

Right now, I'm not sure where I will find my home by the end of our pages together. Some pieces are still moving, and I have no idea where I will land next.

But maybe God has something deeper than a physical home to offer us.

Wherever you are right now, God has something good for you.

I'll confess I roll my eyes a little when people say we are not supposed to feel at home, because this world is not our home (And I get particularly annoyed when they pull out that C.S. Lewis quote about being "made for another world."[6]) It doesn't make me feel any better to know that.

But it does change my perspective.

The things and even the feelings we long for won't fix that ache. No matter how much we want them to.

Wherever you are right now, God has something good for you.

A friend texted me today saying she finally reached a goal weight she had worked toward since age sixteen. After ten years of striving to hit a number on a scale she thought would make everything better, she said, "It doesn't feel as good as I thought it would."

My heart sank because I know that disappointment all too well. We chase that elusive thing we believe will make us better, but even when we attain it, it's just never enough.

As I responded to her, I thought about you too. I wonder, what are you running so hard after? What new circumstance do you believe will change everything?

I don't need to tell you that, just as my friend experienced, reaching your milestone probably won't feel as good as you thought it would. Part of me suspects you already know that since you are here.

So what do we do in the middle? When we still have something we want so badly?

We are heading toward that conversation. But before we wrap up this chapter, I want to leave you with three truths to remember:

You aren't the only one.

You are where you are supposed to be.

You don't have to catch up.

It's okay if you don't believe those words just yet. Some days, I don't know if I'm fully convinced either. But at other moments, I find myself fully confident that God is working everything out *for me*. Not just for everyone else, but for *my* life. Even when it looks like the opposite.

The same is true for you. Now, let's unpack how to live like we believe he is who he says he is.

You aren't the only one.
You are where you are supposed to be.
You don't have to catch up.

CHAPTER 4

Is This My Punishment?

NOT THAT LONG ago, my life looked anything but godly. I spent my college years like a walking stereotype: the Goody Two-shoes Christian girl who goes to college, joins a sorority, and turns into a party girl.

I spent many nights drinking to the point of not remembering everything that happened, then many mornings spiraling in shame and nursing a hangover. I starved my body, overworked it at the gym, and gave it away to the guy I dated in order to feel worthy and loved.

While that's a condensed version of that story, the point is, I have quite a few things in my past I'm not proud of. I made choices that caused me and others a lot of pain and heartbreak, and I made mistakes I sometimes wish I could undo.

You're not reading a book by a gal who has done it all right. In fact, you're reading a book by a gal whose past should disqualify her from writing a book about God at all.

For years, I lived in shame.

I censored details from my past depending on who I was talking to. I worried if anyone knew the real me, they would write me off. When I compared my past to others, mine seemed so much worse.

And when I slipped back into old habits and patterns, I beat myself up for days after.

If you've ever felt this way, you are not alone. In the midst of all the hiding or even self-hatred, you can easily start to believe God can't redeem any of it. Then you may wonder if your circumstances are a direct result of what you've done—that you have made your bed and now have to lie in it. But that's not true.

Though shame threatens to steal from your past, it does not get the final say in your story.

What is that thing you are afraid to mention out loud?

The thing you regret most and wish you could undo?

The thing that still makes you feel guilty?

The thing that makes you think, *If they knew about this, they would never love me*?

Personally, I could name a few things, so I've spent a lot of time fearing I had totally screwed up my life—that whatever good plan God had made for me was no longer an option because of the choices I made.

When something bad happens, or when I'm feeling behind compared to those who seem to be moving right along in life, I usually find myself wondering: *Is this my punishment?*

Am I not where I want to be in life because of my past?

Is this my fault?

Writing those words feels a little dark, but if we're being honest with each other, don't we secretly have those thoughts?

Though shame threatens to steal from your past, it does not get the final say in your story.

THE GOSPEL IS STILL TRUE FOR YOU

Even though I knew what the Bible said about God's grace and forgiveness, I didn't always believe it applied to me. I mean, I did in theory, but my mind (and the enemy) can be quick to tell me otherwise. Ephesians 2:8 says we're only saved by grace through faith and not of our own works. But I found myself working hard to make sure I was good enough anyway. I thought because I messed up, there would be big consequences. Ones that matched the level of my sin.

While nothing immediately happened, I feared the consequences that would appear down the road.

For example, because I went too far physically with my college boyfriend, I feared I would never get married. I truly thought I was doomed to singleness for the rest of my days.

Or at best, I'd eventually get married, but my marriage would have problems because of the choices I made in that college relationship. The Bible makes no such claim, but somewhere along the way I picked up that wrong way of thinking.

These trains of thought led to lots of regret. I assumed if we had never dated, or if we hadn't made mistakes, then my life would've looked different. Maybe I would have gotten married to a nice guy I met right out of college instead of spending the rest of my twenties single.

Which is *a lot* of weight to put on myself!

Then there are other decisions that felt life-altering and I wonder what would have happened if I had chosen differently. If I had gotten a different job out of school, would I have made more money or grown more successful? Had I moved to a different city, how different would my life have looked?

Would I still feel so behind?

Maybe for you the issue is not some big mistake from your past but the small daily choices you face. You find yourself wanting so badly to do the right thing, to earn God's favor and approval, that you are afraid of making the wrong choice and messing up your life. Your walk with God has become a list of things you do out of fear rather than out of a genuine desire to know him in a deeper way.

As we grow in our relationships with God, it's natural for our desires to shift toward his. It's a good thing to want to honor and please him. We're heading toward that conversation in chapter 6.

God invites us to participate in what he's doing, but he doesn't expect us to perform (see James 2:22).

Trying to earn his love through what we do doesn't work. Nothing we can accomplish on our own makes us worthy.

God invites us to participate in what he's doing, but he doesn't expect us to perform.

HOW GOOD THINGS CAN HAPPEN TO BAD PEOPLE

If you find yourself asking:

"Did I not seek God enough?"

"Am I not growing enough?"

"Do I need to do more?"

You may have adopted a belief system that theologians call *retribution theology*.

I know that's a big term. Trust me, the first time I studied it, the words kind of made my head spin. But hang with me. Understanding this belief system can clear up a lot of confusion about God and how he does (and does not) work.

The simplest definition of retribution theology I can give you after studying it is this:

> When bad things happen to people who act or behave in bad, negative, or unethical ways. In other words, people receive punishment for their sins.[1]

According to retribution theology, good things happen to good people and bad things happen to bad people. So if something bad happens to a person, we can assume they must have done something bad to cause it. (That's what *retribution* means.)

Which, by the way, is not the gospel. This way of thinking contradicts what the Bible says is true. Look at Job or Paul, for example. God said Job was "blameless and upright," and he still lost everything (Job 1:1). Then Paul dedicated his life to telling people about Jesus but spent most of it in prison (see Acts 16).

We think our mistakes deserve punishment—and they do (Romans 6:23). However, Jesus took on that punishment for us (2 Corinthians 5:21).

This may be harder to reconcile because we often *want* to believe that bad things will happen to bad people. On the flip side, we hope good things will happen to good people.

Do the right things, make the right choices, and you guarantee life will go your way.

But that's not how life works. That is a belief in karma. And despite what Taylor Swift has to say about it, karma is not real.

One plus one does not always equal two in God's math. But how desperately do we wish it did?

It would be a whole lot easier to have control over our lives if God worked this way every single time. He does sometimes, but not all the time. We see this in the Bible and we see it today. Let's imagine a hypothetical person who tries really hard at work. They do all the right things and seem motivated, so they get the promotion they deserve. On the flip side, another person is lazy and cheats the system. They don't treat people well and eventually get fired for something unethical. We are comfortable with those results. They line up with the way we believe the world, and God, should work.

Yet, in reality, the opposite is often true: The person who most deserves the promotion gets passed up for someone who sucked up to the boss but never put in the work to earn it. Or the friend whom you know would be the best mom can't get pregnant, yet the friend who wasn't even trying does. Or the person who obsessively wants to get married manages to find someone, while the friend who quietly longs for it and patiently waits on God's timing doesn't meet anyone year over year.

When this happens, we often ask questions. *Is it something I did? Or something I'm not doing?*

Then, when our *why* questions aren't answered, we start to question *who* God really is.

Is he really kind? Does he have good plans for me? Why is he withholding what I want so badly? Does he not care?

When doing all the right things doesn't lead to the outcomes we want, we can develop wrong ideas about God. It's easy to treat him like a vending machine: If we put in the right actions, words, and motivations, we should get exactly what we want.

But what if what we want is not actually God's best?

What if God is withholding what we want because we are trying to build a kingdom that is not his?

That is a tough pill to swallow—mostly because it means admitting our longings aren't aligned with his. More than that, it means acknowledging we have tried to become great apart from him.

You may have heard the story of the Tower of Babel, when the people of Genesis 11 tried to build a kingdom for themselves. These people decided to build a tower to the heavens in order to make themselves great and like God. In short, they made a huge mess of things, and as a result, God caused them all to speak different languages. They scattered in confusion to different parts of the world. Once a unified people who spoke one common language, God separated them.

Can you imagine? Not only did they fail to finish the tower, but they also could no longer understand what people they knew and loved were saying.

Crazy story, right? But what does that mean for you and me?

If we peel back the layers, I think we will find God not withholding because he is cruel but because he is kind.

Our circumstances may seem unfair, but what if God is actually preventing us from becoming like Satan? I know that is a dramatic question, but think about it! In Ezekiel 28:15-18, we see Satan being kicked out of heaven because he became prideful and thought he no longer needed God. When we try to center our lives around our wants and needs and keep God on the sidelines as we do it, we are doing what Satan did. We'll talk more about that later, but it's important to acknowledge it now.

What we see as preventing our happiness is actually God protecting us from getting hurt.

You might be in a moment right now where you do feel hurt. Really hurt. What you are going through does not feel like God's protection in the slightest. We are going to talk a lot about that in the next few chapters.

Submission to God's will is not something he blindly expects from us. In fact, Jesus himself submitted to God's plan and will (Luke 22:42).

Our job is obedience, and God's job is the outcome.

Believe it or not, this is comforting news for us. It means we don't have to try so dang hard. It's exhausting to put the weight of it all on our shoulders when it was never meant to be our burden to carry.

We can live free from striving. We don't have to make up for our mistakes.

Our job is obedience, and God's job is the outcome.

WE DON'T HAVE TO STRIVE

As I've worked on this chapter, I've struggled to believe any of this is true for me. Not only because of my past, but also because of situations happening right now as I write. I've feared that the choices I'm making aren't going to lead to the results I want—that if anything goes wrong or sideways, it will be my fault.

Those old ways of thinking have crept back in. Apparently, I still need to untangle some of the false beliefs of retribution theology that I've wrestled with for so long.

I think deep down I'm trying to make my days count in order to make up for how I used to live. I want God to be proud of me for how I'm living now. After almost a decade, I still want to make up for lost time.

Because what I am really afraid of is his judgment. I fear that the grace I'm given in Christ is not enough—that I will be punished for what I've done wrong. That maybe God is going to be mad at me.

Not every angle of this thinking is wrong. According to the Bible, isn't fearing God the beginning of wisdom?

> The fear of the LORD is the beginning of wisdom,
> and knowledge of the Holy One is understanding
> (Proverbs 9:10).

> He said to the human race, "The fear of the LORD—
> that is wisdom, and to shun evil is understanding"
> (Job 28:28).

The fear of the LORD is the beginning of wisdom;
all who follow his precepts have good understanding.
To him belongs eternal praise (Psalm 111:10).

But fearing God is not about being afraid; fearing God means standing in awe. To be reminded of how big and great and wonderful God really is.

In Christ we are free from God's judgment.

He took on our sins—past, present, and future—so we can have a relationship with God that never ends (Romans 5). We don't have to be afraid of God; we get to be close to him.

> ## Fearing God is not about being afraid; fearing God means standing in awe.

Maybe you're reading this and questioning if you really are in Christ. If that's the case, the most important thing you can do is flip to the back of this book and read the "How to Know Jesus Personally" section on page 199. It will change everything about where we head from here.

HOW TO FIGHT THE LIES WE BELIEVE

Whether it's because of something we were taught or told, we can start to believe the lie that one wrong decision can derail the rest of our lives.

Our choices do yield to temporary setbacks but that doesn't mean that we're forever, permanently, and perpetually behind. Life may look different, but life can still be good.

Our choices have consequences, and sometimes those are deeply painful. But that doesn't mean God's plans for our lives are ruined. He can still redeem every part of them.

Even when we read stories in the Bible about people who really messed up, we see God's restoration. One of my favorite examples of this is the story of King David and Bathsheba in 2 Samuel 11. While David was supposed to be on the battlefield fighting with his men, he stayed home. Then he noticed a beautiful (and married) woman named Bathsheba, sent a messenger to summon her to him, and got her pregnant. To cover it up, David had her husband killed. As a result, God did not allow their baby to live. In 2 Samuel 12, we see how this loss caused David unimaginable pain.

But even after his grievous sins and their tragic consequences, David is still called "a man after [God's] own heart" (1 Samuel 13:14). His next child with Bathsheba was Solomon, who became one of the greatest kings to ever rule (1 Kings 4:29-34). And David, Bathsheba, and Solomon are all included in the lineage of Jesus (Matthew 1:6).

David's sin led to suffering, but God didn't allow the story to stop there. He continued to use this family in great ways.

Our choices do yield to temporary setbacks but that doesn't mean that we're forever, permanently, and perpetually behind.

Suffering is what we experience on this side of heaven because things are not how God intended them to be. In a way, feeling behind is actually a symptom of our fallen world. When we feel like we did something to delay or detour our lives, we are feeling a sense of "Life is not what it should be."

But shame tells us we need to punish ourselves.

In heaping judgment on ourselves, we dismiss what Jesus already did on our behalf. Romans 8:1 says, "Therefore, there is now no condemnation for those who are in Christ Jesus."

That means in Christ, you are free from having to hide in shame.

While we can know in our heads that is what the Bible says, it feels more challenging to believe in our hearts that it is true.

So what do we do with all of this? If we find ourselves stuck in shame or believing we have to earn the things we long for, where do we go from here?

We return to what is true. We open our Bibles and find out what God has to say about the lies we believe. I've found three simple steps to do this:

1. Acknowledge something is a lie. If it contradicts God's Word, it's not true. Sometimes we need a friend's help, so send the text or make the phone call and ask someone if what you're believing is a lie.

2. Replace the lie with what the Bible says is true. (And there's *no* shame in googling to find a verse if you don't know where to look.)

3. Repeat God's words over and over until they feel real. Which sometimes feels crazy, but eventually the words will stick. Then the next time the lie creeps back in, the truth will more quickly come to mind.

That's it. If the enemy whispers in your ear that this is your fault, that you've missed your opportunity, or that it's too late to change, you can tell him and yourself what's true:

God is bigger than you (Isaiah 40:22).

His plan does not change based on your decisions (Proverbs 16:9).

He is sovereign (Colossians 1:17).

He loves to redeem the past and our mistakes (Ephesians 1:7-9).

If you told me at 21 that one day I'd be writing a book describing the moments I regretted most, I would have thought you were crazy. But I'm not just writing about those moments; I'm writing about them without feeling regret.

Which may sound even crazier, but it's true. While yes, those decisions caused others and me a lot of hurt and harm, I don't know if I would take them back. Not because I'd choose to relive them, but because I wouldn't be here with you right now. Telling you that there's hope. That God is still writing a story for your life that is good.

I would have missed so much. I never would have worked for a college ministry and gotten to pour into girls who were in the same spot I was in while in college. I would have missed out on traveling overseas to give people access to clean drinking water. I would never have experienced true grace and forgiveness. I would have been judgmental, sad, lonely, and lost. I probably would have continued making choices that were destructive to me and those around me.

**God is bigger than you.
His plan does not change based on
your decisions. He is sovereign.
He loves to redeem the
past and our mistakes.**

The moment I finally gave up and told God I would do anything he asked me to do, everything changed.[2]

And if I hadn't surrendered, I would have missed my life.

It's the crazy, doesn't make sense, upside-down grace of an empty grave that turns the most broken things into beautiful ones. I'm in awe that the most messed-up parts of our stories can actually be used to give God even an ounce of glory.

Could my life have looked different if I hadn't made those choices? Absolutely. But I'll never know that life. And I've made peace with that because I trust God to work everything out. He has so far, and when I read my Bible, I see proof of it over and over.

That's what he does. And I'm thankful.

This part is crucial before we move on. I want to go there with you because the enemy would love nothing more than for you to sideline yourself because of your past sins and mistakes. The lies he whispers, telling you that you are behind, and the reasons are all your fault makes me want to fight back.

It's not true! Period.

You need to believe that. If you get nothing else out of this book, I pray you get this: No matter how bad, shocking, or gross your past or current sin seems, God loves you too much to leave you feeling shame. When you surrender your life to Jesus, there is no more room for shame (Romans 8:28). It does not belong, and you can live free.

No matter what we've done, when we run to Jesus and put our faith in him, he provides a place for us. A place where we are no longer the guilty ones but the righteous ones because of his righteousness. A place where we are safe from the consequences of sin and death.

He provides a way out for every mistake and every intentional wrong if we confess and repent of our sin (1 John 1:8-9).

Friend, this is the best news. No matter what you've done, regardless of your past mistakes, Jesus offers a refuge. He has prepared a place (John 14:1-3). There is no wrong you have done that cannot be forgiven. He is safe. All you have to do is run to him. He is closer than you think.

If we were sitting across the table from each other at a coffee shop, I'd tell you all about it again: all the things I thought I'd never be able to say out loud, much less say without feeling ashamed. I'd recall how many times I thought I had messed up too much for God to love me.

Then I'd tell you about the small ways Jesus pursued my heart until he eventually got louder than I could ignore. I'd pull out my first journal with the pink flowers on it, the one that is tearstained and well-worn. I'd show you how he radically changed my life between my junior and senior years of college.

I might get a little teary as I reflect on all he has done to rescue me from myself, and how he continues to rescue me now, even years later. And then I'd look you in the eye and say, "He can do the same for you."

God takes messed up people and accomplishes his purposes through them anyway.

So here is my challenge as we end this chapter: Say the thing you are afraid to say out loud. To God, to a friend, or to a counselor. Say it aloud because that's not who you are anymore.

When you live like you've been redeemed, living in the light and inviting others to do the same gets a whole lot easier. The enemy knows you're dangerous to him if you're no longer in the dark. And you, my friend, were made to bring light.

CHAPTER 5

You Might Always Grieve What Did (or Did Not) Happen

JULY 2022

I stood in the back of the dark auditorium during worship. It was the last session of the annual summer conference we have for work, and I just wanted it to be over. For two days I had managed to block out my emotions and show up with a smile. Inside, I felt physically exhausted and emotionally weary. With my arms crossed, I listened as the band sang "Goodness of God" by Bethel Music.

The lyrics felt anything but true to me in that moment. In fact, they almost seemed unfair.

I looked around at the room full of women, singing with their hands raised—but I couldn't see the goodness of God. His goodness did not seem to be "running after me." And he certainly didn't feel faithful to me.

The day before the conference started, the guy I was dating had ended things very abruptly. He didn't give me an explanation, and I was driving myself crazy trying to figure out what went wrong. The breakup left me with many questions and little closure.

I'm not one to get too excited about a boy. In fact, I usually try to protect my heart by not letting myself get excited at all. But this boy had seemed different. He checked many boxes, even boxes I didn't know I had. I'd told my friends he seemed too good to be true, and that only made things worse. Because they encouraged me not to assume the worst.

Earlier in the year, almost the same thing had happened: A seemingly great guy I went on a few dates with suddenly ended it and didn't give me a reason why. That time, it didn't take me long to find peace with it, but it still stung.

This time, I was truly disappointed. More than that, I was mad at God.

I know a breakup (if you can even call it that) may seem like a dramatic reason to get mad at God, but I was so tired of the cycle of growing hopeful only to be let down. Mostly because I didn't feel like I was seeking it out. As I stood in the back of the auditorium, I told God I didn't want to keep doing this.

I didn't want to keep getting my hopes up only to get disappointed.

Even the timing of it all had felt too good to be true. With my thirtieth birthday on the horizon, I was struggling to believe God would give me someone to spend the rest of my life with before I entered a new decade. So when someone appeared right as the decade was entering its final six months, it hurt even more when it didn't work out. Hope restored, then hope snatched away. Again.

The next day my friend Victoria and I went on a walk to debrief. She listened like a good friend does, and then she said, "I just feel like this has happened to you a lot, and I'm sorry. It does not feel fair, and I don't know why. But it's kind of like rolling your ankle on a run. The first couple of times, you can just run through it and shake it off. At some point, though, after you've rolled it enough times, you're injured. And you can't run through an injury, you have to stop and let it heal. I think you're injured, Meghan, and you need to figure out how to stop and heal."

She was right. I couldn't keep moving. But I had no idea what healing looked like.

THE IMPORTANCE OF A FUNERAL

The unlikely first step to healing is grieving.

I wouldn't have recognized grieving as the first step, but my friend Lysa TerKeurst has taught me a lot about the necessity of it. A few years ago, she shared her idea of having what she calls "mini funerals" for our disappointments.[1] Whether a circumstance didn't turn out the way you wanted, or a person let you down even when your expectations for them were realistic, disappointment can set in. Left unattended to, those disappointments can lead to hurt, bitterness, and distrust.

Pausing and giving ourselves time to mourn the things that didn't meet our expectations, however, helps us avoid the bitterness that comes from unhealed hurts.

We don't often talk about the grief that comes with disappointment. Actually, we don't talk about grief a lot, period—likely because we don't want to, but also because we don't know how.

Grief does not just accompany a physical death; it also accompanies the death of a relationship or the death of a dream. Grief signals that something has not turned out the way we want or think it should be. Friend, being let down is painful, and rightfully so.

I'm not sure if the circumstances that led you to pick up this book involve the physical death of someone. If they did, I'm so sorry. Tears come to my eyes as I write this thinking about the loss you may be feeling, and I wish I could simply sit with you. I'm honored you would trust me in this journey.

Pausing and giving ourselves time to mourn the things that didn't meet our expectations, however, helps us avoid the bitterness that comes from unhealed hurts.

I went to a funeral a few weeks ago. I didn't know the person that well, but as I walked alongside someone who did, I thought about how we tend to rush through grief. After a loved one's death, the family has little time to plan a funeral and arrange the details of burial. Then, a few short days after the funeral, the family members go back to work, expected to move on as if nothing happened.

Until we've experienced loss, we don't know how it feels. But even as outsiders, we understand how wrong their losses are. Life as they knew it has been stolen; how does anyone recover from that? Let alone show up for normalcy right afterward?

Grief also comes in waves. Time can help dull the pain, but it never completely goes away. Sometimes grief is triggered out of nowhere, and the pain feels as fresh as its first wound. The hurt is unpredictable, no matter what you do to avoid it.

In Jewish culture, they have a practice called sitting *shiva*[2]. In Hebrew, *shiva* means "seven," which is the number of days the immediate family spends mourning a deceased loved one. For seven days after the burial, the family stays home together and focuses on their loss as a part of their healing. But that is just the first step; the grieving process moving forward takes years.

I think there's value in creating the space to process and mourn.

Yet so often we are expected to move on too quickly. As we try to keep moving or avoid pain, we also try to numb it and ignore it. In my life, moving on looks like pretending it didn't happen. I've subconsciously believed that if I don't allow myself to sit in my sadness or anger too long, the pain will go away.

When we try to numb our pain, we also numb the possibility of our healing.

No one is comfortable with pain. Who *wants* to feel pain? Or struggle? Certainly not me!

However, in our grief, we are more available to experience comfort and kindness.[3]

Even more in our grief, we are most available to experience God's presence.

Quick time-out here: As I stood in the back of that auditorium, and even as I went on a walk with my friend, the previous two sentences would not have made me feel any better. In fact, I might have resented them. Knowing God could comfort me in my pain was not the problem; the problem was I knew he could change my situation, yet he'd chosen not to. This knowledge only increased my frustration and made me question if he was really the loving God I thought he was.

When we try to numb our pain, we also numb the possibility of our healing.

For a long time, I didn't think I could express that out loud. I felt like a bad Christian and thought I should know better. Other people appeared to handle their disappointments more gracefully than I did on the inside. But in not expressing those frustrations and questions, I grew more attached to the lie that God was not who the Bible and other people told me he was. I didn't open myself up to his comfort, kindness, and presence because I didn't trust his heart toward me.

You don't have to hide your frustration and questions here. You have a friend here who understands all those emotions. More than that, God can handle your honesty. In fact, he welcomes it (Psalm 139:1-3).

You don't have to show up with clean thoughts and polished

emotions. Have you read any of the psalms? No offense to David, but some of them get kind of dark!

> Why, LORD, do you stand far off? Why do you hide yourself in times of trouble? (Psalm 10:1).

> My life is consumed by anguish and my years by groaning; my strength fails because of my affliction, and my bones grow weak (Psalm 31:10).

What I find interesting about these verses is that David always started his psalms with honest emotion, but eventually turned his thoughts back to what was true about God.

> You, God, see the trouble of the afflicted; you consider their grief and take it in hand. The victims commit themselves to you; you are the helper of the fatherless (Psalm 10:14).

> How abundant are the good things that you have stored up for those who fear you, that you bestow in the sight of all, on those who take refuge in you (Psalm 31:19).

In David's most desperate moments, he reminded himself of who God is. When he was experiencing heartbreak or drowning in fear, he wrote of God's comfort and kindness toward him. He recalled what God had already done in his life and clung to the hope that he would rescue him from despair again.

We can be both honest about the pain of disappointment and hopeful that God can change it. We struggle to find a category that both can be true at the same time.

Hoping seems scary when we have felt constantly disappointed. When we have experienced repeated losses and letdowns, our hurt can lead to wounds that feel incurable. When you doubt your circumstances can ever change, healing seems impossible.

But we should not forget that God moves, exists, and creates outside our framework of understanding. God is the first and best

Creator. His nature is creative (Genesis 1:1). Therefore, he is constantly making things new.

Newness goes beyond what we know and see.

We can be both honest about the pain of disappointment and hopeful that God can change it.

Which is why hope is something hardwired in our hearts and minds by God. Hope goes against our rational thinking and logic as we trust God to do something new. We can't see any solutions to our problems or answers to our questions that exist beyond our own human capabilities. If we can't figure it out, it feels impossible. And that feeling creates anxiety in us.

Hope is *in* us—not only for things we can imagine, but also for things beyond our wildest dreams.

When we stop hoping, we stop healing. And if we stop healing, we will lose hope.

CURING THE INCURABLE

I listened to an episode of the podcast *The Place We Find Ourselves* recently. The episode was called "Is Hope Reasonable?" If that's not the question we are trying to answer, I don't know what is! I couldn't take notes fast enough when I was listening, and I've continued thinking a lot about it.

In the episode, the host talks about how God spoke to the Israelites while they were in exile. They had been taken from their homes, had to live under a tyrant king in an unfamiliar place, and had no idea how long they would have to be there. In the middle of their pain, grief, and suffering, God told his people they had an incurable wound (Jeremiah 30:12). Not exactly comforting, is it? But a few verses later, he spoke the good news: "I will restore you to health and heal your wounds" (Jeremiah 30:17).

Wait, how is that possible? Think back to what we talked about earlier: We can hold our heartbreak and hope together. We can have an "incurable wound" that only God himself can cure. Maybe we cannot fix things, but God can.

You can acknowledge how you feel *and* hope for what's ahead.[4]

God wanted to tell his people that only he could create something new, right at the moment when newness was nowhere in sight. His words reminded them—and they remind us today—that God is free to create newness amid chaos and despair. Furthermore, God is also committed to newness. He says so in his Word, and we see him making things new all over Scripture. He begins in the garden of Eden (Genesis 1). Then he opens barren wombs, including Sarah's (Genesis 18:10), Rebekah's (Genesis 25:21), Rachel's (Genesis 30:22), and much later, the womb of Hannah, mother of the prophet Samuel (1 Samuel 1:19-20). He frees slaves in Egypt (Exodus 6), and he brings his people out of exile (Ezra 1). Ultimately, he sends his Son, Jesus, as a baby to save us (John 1). God has a reputation for doing the impossible.

The stories of the Bible demonstrate the fulfillment of God's promises. But do we believe God will keep his promises to us when all we can see is hopelessness?

What if our thinking is too small, too limited?

Do we have space in our imaginations for something new to happen in us, not because we can make it happen, but because God can do it?

While the Israelites were in exile, the various prophets instructed them to do three things. These directions can also help us walk through grief and experience healing:

1. *Honestly acknowledge the depth of our wounds.* Denying, numbing, or running from what has hurt us keeps us stuck. We have to stop brushing off the pain from life not looking the way we wanted it to. If it hurts, it's because it's painful. We have to acknowledge the reality of where we are.

2. *Grieve the wounds.* Let yourself cry. Don't ignore the ways your body is responding to the pain you are experiencing. Allow yourself to feel. Don't judge yourself or try to fix it. Just grieve.

3. *Risk imagining a newness that only God could create.* God is not confined to rearranging only what's in front of you. He has repeatedly made life and goodness out of nothing. When we are tempted to push all hope from our hearts in order to avoid being disappointed again, we can take a risk and choose hope again. We don't have to manipulate our hopes to heal. In fact, doing so will only hurt us more. We can dream of a life better than the one we have because God can create that for us.

Acceptance. Grief. Hope. They all are required steps in healing. When we are feeling behind, we get to experience a tenderness with God that we would never have experienced otherwise. It's amid seasons of deep grief that he is closest to us. When we get to know him in that way, he creates an intimacy with us we can carry into the future.

We don't have to manipulate our hopes to heal.

Just this past week, a close friend lost her dad unexpectedly. I don't totally know where she stands with God and faith in Jesus at this moment, and I've prayed for years for her to know him deeply. What do you say to a grieving person who isn't totally sure about God? She knows where I stand, so I know I can speak freely. But while we were texting, she told me that prayer and God were the only things giving her any comfort amid immense grief.

He is so close to the grieving (Psalm 34:18). Regardless of what your circumstances are, he promises his presence and an opportunity to know him better.

You might always grieve what did (or did not) happen in your life. But our minds cannot begin to fathom the ways God will restore us.

THE POWER OF GIVING UP

Back to me in July, post-breakup: I wish I could say I did all of these things after Victoria pointed out that I needed to heal. Instead, I did the opposite of the three steps I just listed. I gave up. I wondered if any of the things I claimed to know about God were real. I questioned if I had spent my entire adult life insulating myself with godly things without really knowing God himself.

Which completely terrified me. If I wasn't fully convinced my relationship with God was real, what had I given my life to?

The weeks that followed included a lot of doubt. The few and sporadic days I managed to journal about my thoughts were short and obviously distant. Those entries featured a lot of questions and not a lot of answers.

Then one day, I finally wrote this:

> God, I'm done being mad at you. And I'm sorry for being mad at you. Something about being mad at you feels better than not. Please forgive me. Even now, I feel a resistance to ask you for forgiveness. I feel a lot of

things. Mostly, I'm afraid because I have so much doubt. Doubt and lack of trust. The lies I'm believing don't feel like lies at all. They seem true...I'm too far in to quit you now, and I have nowhere else to go. I'm ashamed this all feels like a house of cards and I'm questioning if I really believe everything I say I do. Was any of this real? Or did I just surround myself with "Christian things" that weren't personal to me? I don't want to stay here, so show me the way out. Help me overcome my unbelief.

Nothing changed in that moment. My heart didn't catch up to my words. Yet day by day, little by little, hope started to rise again.

As I flip through that same journal, I can now see a little flame lit in the weeks and months that followed this entry. By the fall of that year, I felt more convinced that God was worth putting my hope in.

My slight crisis of faith may have been the catalyst to the healing my heart desperately needed.

Maybe you're there right now. You read those words in my journal and they resonate with you. And you're not sure you're quite ready to surrender those emotions of anger and sadness to the Lord. Maybe being mad at God feels easier.

He can handle your emotions. And my invitation to you is to take a few minutes to be honest with him. Pull out a journal or open a note on your phone and just let the words out. Don't try to filter or polish them. Let it all out. Don't put pressure on yourself to fix what you feel; just take a step toward the healing your heart needs.

WE HAVE HOPE

Friend, I want to give you good news: Grief ends.

Revelation 21:4 says, "He will wipe every tear from their eyes.

There will be no more death or mourning or crying or pain, for the old order of things has passed away."

We can remain hopeful—not because we will get everything we want but because the pain we experience in the meantime will not last forever. Grief's end is coming.

Right after God promises to end mourning and pain, he says this:

> He who was seated on the throne said, *"I am making everything new!"* Then he said, "Write this down, for these words are trustworthy and true" (Revelation 21:5, emphasis added).

The second-to-last chapter of the Bible reminds us we have a reason to hope. The best kind of *new* is on the way.

Believe it or not, a week after I stood with arms crossed in the back of that auditorium, I pitched this book's concept to my editor. In the middle of wondering if I even believed God was real, and feeling more behind than ever before, I very hesitantly made good on what I committed myself to. I had no hope anything would come of my pitch. If God was real, and if this dream of writing a book was something he put in me and wanted for me, opening the door would be up to him. I was barely convinced of the topic of the book myself, but something in me needed to see it through.

What I never saw coming was that at my lowest moment, he was creating newness my imagination could not see. But first, I had to experience the kind of comfort, kindness, and presence that could only come through grief.

Then I had to get honest about what I really wanted…but more on that in the next chapter.

CHAPTER 6

What Do I *Really* Want?

JUNE 2022

I shifted in my seat. Crossing my right leg over my left didn't feel comfortable, but the reverse didn't feel right either. To make it worse, the backs of my semi-sweaty legs stuck to the leather chair as I moved around. As I fidgeted with the hair tie around my wrist, Tim, my pastor, offered me a cup of coffee. I declined. I already felt anxious and didn't need caffeine to heighten it.

"What did you want to talk about today?" he asked me kindly from his chair on the other side of the room. I took a deep breath to collect my thoughts.

I needed some pastoral wisdom on a situation that had recently come up with a friend. But I knew deep down my questions weren't just about this situation. The conflict had just kicked an anthill, and my emotions were all over the place. I needed help figuring out what to do now that I couldn't clean up the mess.

Starting with the simple facts, I explained to him what had transpired over the previous 48 hours—how I thought it would impact my day-to-day, but also how it might impact things relationally. Tim listened intently and waited for me to finish. Then he asked me: "If you could use one word to describe how you are feeling, what would it be?"

I blurted out, *"Untethered."*

I don't know where that word came from, but it clearly described what I felt because I hardly had to think about it.

When he asked me to explain further, I took a deep breath and said, "I don't feel attached to anything. I really don't know what to cling to outside of the Lord. And even that feels hard lately. I don't feel at home anywhere. I'm alone. And I'm just…so…tired."

Cue the tears I'd so desperately tried to hold in.

I didn't know what attaching myself to anything even looked like. My job, the city I lived in, the people I called friends…everything seemed a little unstable. Plus, a lot of it seemed attached to other people's decisions.

After we talked some more, Tim suggested I work on finding what he called "rocks" to anchor myself to—things I can commit to regardless of what happens. He pointed out that when we challenge ourselves to commit to something despite any changing circumstances, we can find a sense of comfort and stability. Knowing those rocks won't move even if something unexpected happens helps life feel a little less out of control.

One of his rocks was Charlotte, North Carolina. No matter what, he and his family were committed to staying in Charlotte for at least ten years. They could rest knowing they would stay in the city. He came to this decision through prayer and wise counsel in his life.

When you think about it, for much of history, people committed to things for a lifetime. A few generations ago, most people met their spouses in the town they grew up in, worked the same job for the duration of their careers, and didn't know about much going on outside of their own town unless it showed up on the nightly news.[1]

There's value in commitment we miss out on.

CHANGING OUR PERSPECTIVE

Today we move to different states, switch jobs approximately every three years, and have access to everyone we've ever met and knowledge of what is going on in the rest of the world in our pockets 24-7.

It's no wonder our lives feel untethered and out of control. We don't commit to things for the long haul.

While there is so much freedom that we get to experience as we make choices and change our minds, that freedom can sometimes paralyze us.

How can we possibly commit to one thing when we have so many options?

When Tim challenged me to pick some rocks—things that would not change—I didn't know what to choose. From my perspective, even the rocks I wanted to pick still seemed movable.

For example: The neighborhood I lived in meant a lot to me. I had two of my closest friends living a few doors down. Plus, as we'd made more friends, we'd started getting together for monthly dinners. Our group text always had people asking to borrow things from each other or last-minute plans open to whoever could join. It had created a lot of safety and security in a city far away from each of our families. If I had it my way, we'd all live there forever.

But a few things made it difficult to pick the neighborhood as one of my rocks. My roommate owned the house we lived in, and she had started dating a guy who lived across the country. If she moved, then I wouldn't be able to stay in the house. However, even if we stayed in the house, one of my other friends could always decide to move. Being single, and not owning a house, I felt like I couldn't choose something so dependent on someone else's decisions to be a rock.

I'm sure there are many similar situations you can think of too. Maybe you're single and really desire to be married, and it seems like everyone is making decisions alongside their spouse and you are alone. Or maybe you want your job to be one of your rocks, but you keep getting beat out for a promotion, and therefore you've started looking around for new jobs so you can move up.

Aside from the ultimate rock that is our faith in Jesus, should we be anchored to the houses we live in? The cities we call home? The jobs we have? The people in our communities?

What should we commit to?

I realized maybe the untethered feeling wasn't about a house or neighborhood or even getting married. Maybe there was a hidden promise in each circumstance I really wanted that could lead to feeling steadier.

What is the thing beneath the thing that I'm truly looking for?

What did I value most in my life? And could I pick rocks based on my values instead?

As I tried to start drilling down on what those rocks should be, I opened my journal and asked myself some more questions. I started to trace those values I wanted to build my life on that were hidden beneath the circumstances I longed for.

I wrote three columns in my journal. I started by scribbling down what I wanted most in the first column. Then I wrote about *why* I wanted each of those things so much. In the last column, I asked God to show me how to find what I valued about the things I wanted and apply them to other areas of my life.

It took some time, but I discovered I could find the internal peace I longed for without anything externally changing.

The original version of this chart in my journal was a lot less polished, but I cleaned it up here so it will make more sense for you:

IDENTIFY THE KEY THINGS YOU WANT THAT YOU DON'T HAVE CONTROL OVER YET:

* marriage
* owning a house in the neighborhood I live in
* a promotion

WHY DO YOU WANT EACH OF THOSE THINGS?

* I want a companion to make decisions with—someone to stay with me even when things change. I don't want to be alone.

* If I own a house, then I don't have to move. I like living near my friends. It makes the city feel smaller and gives me comfort knowing I have people close by. I love getting to do things spontaneously with them.

* I want to be seen as a leader. I want the financial security that comes with a promotion.

HOW CAN YOU TAKE THE REASONS YOU WANT THOSE THINGS AND APPLY THEM TO YOUR LIFE IN AN UNEXPECTED WAY?

* I can invite my friends into decisions I make and ask them to include me in the decisions they make. (For example, if I should spend money to go on a trip or change jobs.) I can work through conflict with friends, even when it's difficult. I can initiate making plans with people.

* I can choose where I live based on people nearby. Whether I move to a new city or a new neighborhood, I can look for ways to deepen relationships with the people around me, even if they are newer friends or strangers.

* I can take opportunities at work and outside of work to lead, even without a title. I also can look for other opportunities to make money through freelancing.

In the back of the book, I've included more charts like this one to help you identify the values you want to build on when things feel untethered or out of control.

It may take some time and prayer, or inviting people close to you into the conversation to answer these questions. But digging into these questions can reveal the goodness God has made available right in front of you.

WHAT YOU HAVE RIGHT IN FRONT OF YOU

Friend, can I tell you a secret? You have more ownership over your life than you think you do. You are not subject to the shifting sands of what is going on around you. You have the ability to change your perspective even when you can't change your circumstances.

If you're anything like me, you may feel some resistance toward the previous sentence. I'm not claiming God is not sovereign or that we are the ones in control. No matter what, there are some things we can't change.

> **You have the ability to change your perspective even when you can't change your circumstances.**

But we do have a part to play. We get to choose whether we want to follow his way or our own. We decide if we want to sit back and let what we don't have become more important than what we do have.

Perspective really can make all the difference. If we can see our lives rightly, we can better live in reality.

In Christ, we are not victims; we are victorious (Romans 8:37). When we are confident God has a plan and Jesus has already overcome the enemy, we stop waiting for life to just happen to us.

Maybe you feel unattached to your job but aren't sure if you want to leave. Ask yourself what you value about your current circumstances. Is it the company you work for? Or is it the skills you get to use? The work you get to do? The type of people you work with? Or the flexibility the job offers? Regardless of whether your job changes, you can anchor yourself in what you value in a work environment.

Maybe you're struggling to decide what your anchor should be because you don't have a family to make decisions with. But what are you searching for in a family? Security? Camaraderie? How can you find that in your current community, in this season? What sort of values do you desire in a family that can be duplicated with your friends?

Does it start with talking to your friends about your values and desires? Or with finding friends who have similar values?

Take a few moments to think about your answers to these questions:

What are you going to fill life with?

What do you want to be known for?

What do you want your life to look like?

If your external circumstances drive your answers, you are never going to love your life. You'll miss so much if you let that happen.

What if God is inviting us to imagine something bigger than ourselves? What if we really can use these rocks to build lives that honor him and impact other people for the growth of his kingdom?

WHAT CONTENTMENT IS AND IS NOT

When we are so focused on what we don't have and can't change, we are likely to become discontent.

If you've been alive for any length of time, you know the feeling of discontentment—the search for something, anything to comfort you, but nothing fully does. The ache for steadiness or security. The desire for everything to be in its proper place. The longing for the assurance that you are, and will be, okay.

Have you ever been hungry, but nothing sounds good? You want to eat and know you need to eat, but you can't quite figure out what food will curb your appetite.

When I met with my pastor, I knew my feelings stemmed from being uncomfortable. What I didn't know was that discomfort and discontentment were connected.

The idea of contentment gets thrown around a lot in Christian circles. If I'm honest, sometimes I get squirmy with the word *contentment*. Maybe it's because I'm single at the time of this writing, and well-meaning people like to tell me, "You'll meet someone once you're truly content." Or maybe it's because, single or not, this contentment thing has always felt like an impossible game to win.

At times I've assumed: *If I want something, I won't get it. But if I don't want something, then I will get it.* Similar to the way I manipulate my hope, I try to manipulate my contentment. If I don't want it or if I'm truly content, maybe then God will give it to me.

Whether I'm longing for a new season, an exciting change, or something deeper, I try to make myself not want it because I've come to believe that's what contentment is all about.

Maybe you've been in a similar situation. You've tried to make yourself *not* want something you deeply desire because you think not wanting it will lead to contentment with what you currently have. But I think we've missed something important: Desire and contentment are not mutually exclusive.

Longing for something doesn't mean never finding rest for your soul.

If I were to define contentment, I'd say: Contentment is an inward trust that God is both good and in control of my life, even when I wish my outward circumstances were different.

In Philippians 4, Paul tells us he learned the secret of contentment, and it's a little unexpected:

> I know what it is to be in need, and I know what it is to have plenty. I have learned the secret of being content in any and every situation, whether well fed or hungry, whether living in plenty or in want. I can do all this through him who gives me strength (Philippians 4:12-13).

Desire and contentment are not mutually exclusive.

What's the secret? To deny our needs and wants? No, Paul didn't fake his contentment. Nor did he find it because his circumstances were perfect. The contentment he found only came from Christ, not his own strength.

Even this sounds a little elusive. How do we find contentment in Christ?

I don't know about you, but I love to think I can do things in my own strength. But I'm not as strong as I think I am. Try as I might, I can't muster up my own contentment.

Contentment means living in God's fullness, which means contentment is possible because it's independent of our circumstances.

We love verses like Ephesians 3:20: "Now to him who is able to do immeasurably more than all we ask or imagine, according to his power that is at work within us."

Immeasurably more than all I can ask or imagine? Sign me up! I'd be super content with that. But the "immeasurably more" isn't found in my life looking the way I want it to. God's fullness looks like verses 14-19:

> For this reason I kneel before the Father, from whom every family in heaven and on earth derives its name. I pray that out of his *glorious riches* he may *strengthen you with power through his Spirit in your inner being,* so that *Christ may dwell in your hearts* through faith. And I pray that you, *being rooted and established in love,* may have power, together with all the Lord's holy people, to grasp how wide and long and high and deep is the love of Christ, and to know this love that surpasses knowledge—that you may be *filled to the measure of all the fullness of God* (emphasis added).

God cares more about our internal being than our external circumstances. Note what Paul calls the fullness of God: strength in your inner being, Christ dwelling in you, rooted and established in love, to grasp the love of Christ, to know his love.

Contentment comes from within.

God's fullness does not change. He is "the same yesterday and today and forever" (Hebrews 13:8).

But this doesn't mean we won't still have desires. You can be content in Christ and still desire for something to be different.

What we do with those desires is what matters. More notably, we need to pay attention to where those desires stem from (which we will talk about in the next chapter).

You can be content in Christ and still desire for something to be different.

WHEN THE CIRCUMSTANCES CHANGE AND WE DON'T WANT THEM TO

January 2023

It's been several months since I sat in Tim's office. As I write today, I'm failing miserably at not manipulating my hope.

For the majority of this week, I've tried to convince myself and everyone around me that I'm fine. But I know full well that I am not.

I've pulled back when people have asked how I'm doing, slapped on a smile, and said, "Things are good, just busy." But inside I'm screaming because everything is about to change. I know that, and there's nothing I can do to control or fix it.

I'm pretty terrible at faking my emotions, so my friends can see right through me. They are giving me time to process alone and being wildly gracious by not pressing too hard. Eventually I will tell them what's going on, but I'm not ready yet.

Part of me hopes that if I keep up appearances, my heart will catch up.

It's the end of January, and we got an unusually warm and sunny day in North Carolina. I started the day a little anxious because so much change is coming. A few months from now, my whole life will look different. In some ways, this is good, but a lot of it is still unknown.

When I came home from work today, Madi officially told me

she's selling the house. I knew it was coming, so the news didn't catch me totally off guard. She's getting married in a few months and moving to San Francisco. An answered prayer in so many ways.

But it's the end of an era. The little home we made is dispersing. We all knew it wasn't meant to last forever, but I'm still sad it's almost over. I don't know if staying in our neighborhood is an option, and if I let myself linger on that thought, it breaks my heart.

I haven't cried yet. But as I type, I can feel it brewing.

I just went on a run, which is definitely a coping mechanism. When I got back, I lay in the middle of our driveway and stared at the sky. I thought about the popcorn ceilings I've spent years looking at. The same questions about God lingered just beneath the surface:

Do I still believe God is loving and kind now that I have to move again?

Do I believe what he has for me next is better than what I have right now?

So far, he has not failed to provide a place for me to live and people for me to live with. I *know* that. But right now, all I feel is sadness. The thought of roommates 20 and 21 makes me so dang tired. And this time, I had really believed I wouldn't end up here.

The space between what I know and what I feel is great. But *who* I know is greater, and that's all I have to stand on.

I desperately hope it's enough.

I'm also dating someone right now, but it's all so new and I have no idea where it's going. I'm hopeful in a way that scares me. But we don't even live in the same city. Something about that reality makes this move and decision feel harder. It's difficult enough not to manipulate my hopes within that relationship; throw all the other changes into the mix, and I feel so out of control.

But I have to remind myself that I'm never in control. I sometimes can have an illusion of being in control, and when I realize it's not reality, that's when I freak out a little.

I don't know why I lay on the ground today and looked at the sky. It's not something I normally do. But stepping out of my little house and looking up reminds me how small I am. In a good way.

The thing about looking at the sky is that it reminds you it's not falling.

The clouds are moving.

The world is still spinning.

And God is still in control.

Maybe all those years of staring at the ceiling limited my perspective because I was only looking at myself, my problems, and my little world. All of which are valid concerns. But I just wasn't looking at them from the right angle.

Right now, I am scared of what's next.

I feel the shifts not just externally but internally too. I don't know what yet, but I can feel in my bones that God is up to something and he's not going to let me in on it until the right moment.

But I have to trust him. What is my other option?

Before I stood up from the driveway, I saw it: a small rainbow, barely visible above me.

The cynical part of me would typically write that off as coincidence, but I know it wasn't. The rainbow has long been a sign of God's faithfulness to keep his promises (Genesis 9:13).

The tears are coming now.

I know he is faithful.

He is still good and kind, even if I have to move ten more times and live with 20 more roommates before I turn 40.

What he has next for me is better than what I have now. It always is. I've seen it time and time again. Just when I thought it couldn't get any better, it did.

When I didn't believe I could love another city more than my hometown, I did.

When I was convinced I had already made the best friends I could ever have, I made new ones.

Every time I've thought what I was leaving behind was the best it could ever be, God proved me wrong.

None of that came without grief or pain, but I've continuously come out the other side better than I started.

Every time I was more convinced that God's faithfulness is my favorite thing about him. He does not change or leave or flake out on us. He is fully committed to keeping every single promise he makes. I am sure of it.

Maybe from now on, I'll go lie on the sidewalk and stare at the sky instead of the ceiling.

And rainbow or not, I'll remember God's faithfulness to me.

CHAPTER 7

Do I Want This Too Much?

APRIL 2023

I remember the day I drove my moving truck across town to Madi's house like it was yesterday. It had started raining. I was already covered in sweat and dirt, death-gripping the steering wheel as I blinked back tears. I begged, and I mean begged, for God to let this be the last time I had to do this alone. Ten houses in ten years, roommates 18 and 19 on deck. I was well past being over it.

Moving was exhausting. I didn't have my dad there to help me. I'd gotten in an argument with the grumpy attendant at the U-Haul pickup spot who tried to make me pay more than I already had. Several friends graciously showed up to help me load and unload, and I felt like the world's biggest inconvenience when they did. It was an epic pity party in the making.

Fast-forward two years, and I'm there again today. I'm not crying, but I'm looking at a house full of boxes, feeling that same disappointment rise again. House 11 and roommates 20 and 21, here I come.

God, I really wanted that to be the last time I had to do this alone.

Did I mention where I am moving? I'm moving into the basement of my friend's parents' house. At 30 years old…I'll be living in someone's basement. It's humbling. At least it's not *my* parents' house. But still.

The Floyds are the most generous people, having offered me a place to land while I figure out what the heck I want to do next. Once again, though, this is not what I thought my next move would be. This move feels worse, actually, because it seems like I'm moving backwards.

On top of that, the guy I'm dating meets my parents this week. Which, until last night, I was pretty excited about. Things have been going really well. But after talking on the phone last night, I'm scared we aren't on the same page. And I'm trying really hard not to spiral out about it.

The conversation wasn't bad or even alarming. We're both doing our best: learning to communicate, figuring out how to navigate conflict—you know, the things you do when you're trying to decide if you want to spend the rest of your life with someone. And when I'm at my best, I can recognize we're in a good spot.

But my heart is already there. While I'm not ready for the next step yet, I know where I want this relationship to go. I'm not sure if these words will make it into the final cut of this book, but even writing them down freaks me out.

I'm terrified of getting hurt. I don't know if I can handle another blow in the relationship department. Okay, I know I can and will if it comes to that, but dang, I really don't want to.

As I look at the boxes piling up in the corner of my living room, I can feel myself looking for something or someone I can cling to for security and assurance. Which is not at all fair to the guy I'm dating. I know I should cling to the Lord, but he's not exactly being forthcoming with me about what's ahead. Therefore, I'm letting what I can't see amplify my insecurities.

I think if I knew for sure that this relationship is headed for marriage, then moving into my friend's parents' basement would be a stepping stone and not a heavy rock attached to my ankle. A stepping stone feels much better—like progress, albeit small progress. But the issue isn't knowing where this relationship is heading so much as needing to sit in the discomfort of this season being temporary.

But I have no idea how long this season will last. Will it be two months? Six months?

We all want to know what God is up to. But in between where we are and where we'd like to be, there's a lot of room for wrestling.

Between doubt and faith.

Between control and surrender.

Between anxiety and peace.

Between cynicism and hope.

Between skepticism and trust.

I want to be firm in my faith, but the minute something feels shaky, I find myself flailing and fragile.

I know in my head God cares about my heart the most. He alone guards and protects me (2 Thessalonians 3:3). So why does my heart have such a hard time believing that?

WHEN WANTS BECOME NEEDS

I *really* want this relationship to work out, and I'm trying to remain hopeful. As we talked about in the last chapter, having desires is not always a bad thing.

But the familiar uneasiness I feel about my lack of control? That's telling me something: My desires have turned into something deeper. I've turned what I want into a need.

Ugh. Not a fun realization, but a true one. The desires we have can quickly become demands we place on God. Which I'll be the first to admit, I do.

Especially when the things we want are good and godly things.

Marriage? The Bible says it's not good for man to be alone (Genesis 2:18).

Children? The Bible says children are a gift from the Lord (Psalm 127:3).

Success after hard work? The Bible says commit to the Lord, and you will succeed (Proverbs 16:3).

(I could go on here.)

But do you know what else the Bible says is true?

Suffering: "Not only so, but we also glory in our sufferings, because we know that suffering produces perseverance; perseverance, character; and character, hope. And hope does not put us to shame, because God's love has been poured out into our hearts through the Holy Spirit, who has been given to us" (Romans 5:3-5).

Persecution: "Blessed are those who are persecuted because of righteousness, for theirs is the kingdom of heaven" (Matthew 5:10).

Singleness: "To the unmarried and the widows I say: It is good for them to stay unmarried, as I do" (1 Corinthians 7:8).

Yeah, yeah, I know, do we really have to talk about those things? Yes, but we can do it! It'll be worth it, I promise.

Because Psalm 34:9-10 has some good news for us:

> Fear the LORD, you his holy people, *for those who fear him lack nothing.* The lions may grow weak and hungry, but those who seek the LORD *lack no good thing* (emphasis added).

When we fear God and seek him, we do not lack. Does anyone besides me have a hard time believing that? When the "good things" I want are out of my reach, this doesn't feel true. It especially doesn't feel true when I think I *need* those good things I don't yet have.

Then, when I can't get those things, I get tired of waiting for them, and before I know it, I'm taking matters into my own hands.

Which never goes well.

Oftentimes, it looks like me stiff-arming God while I pout and throw myself a pity party.

Other times, I seek comfort in anything but him—food, alcohol, spending money, friends, or followers online.

Then sometimes it looks trying to get what I want without his help. Like redownloading the dating apps to try to force something to happen. Or overdoing it at the gym to try to look a certain way. Or applying for more jobs when doors aren't opening.

And I do it without consulting God at all.

It's not *what* we do, as much as it is the reason behind *why* we do them.

This, my friend, is what the Bible calls idolatry. And I'll be the first to raise my hand and admit I struggle with it the most.

In the Old Testament, idolatry involved ascribing to something else what was only due to God (Exodus 20:2-4). To put it more plainly: looking to receive something from another god that only God could give. Over and over, we see the people of God, the Israelites, choosing to worship idols.

Their idolatry came down to a lack of trust in God; they didn't believe he could give them what they needed.

The moment we stop trusting God to be God, we look to ourselves or something else to become a god. In my experience, I'm a really bad god. So are the other people and things I look to be gods.

Which the Israelites also experienced as they wandered in the wilderness...

When God freed Israel from slavery in Egypt, he committed to leading them to the promised land: a place where they would be free and provided for. But amid the change and the unfamiliar, they started to complain. They wanted to go back to Egypt because at least they had food there (Exodus 16:3). In the pain of the unknown, they forgot God's promises and doubted his provision.

(Ouch. Are your toes getting stepped on too?)

But God graciously met them in their complaining (Exodus 16:12). He told them he would provide bread from heaven just for them called manna, which means "What is it?" because they had never tasted it before (Exodus 16:4). But even after God gave them what they asked for, they didn't trust him. They gathered more manna than they needed because they feared he wouldn't send more the next day. Instead of letting God's past provision point them to what he promised for the future, they tried to protect and provide for themselves.

(It's me, hi…anybody else?)

The moment we stop trusting God to be God, we look to ourselves or something else to become a god.

It got worse. When God's people didn't get to the promised land as quickly as they wanted, they decided to fashion idols out of gold to worship the gods of other nations—because maybe those gods would get them where they wanted to go faster. (Exodus 32 tells the whole story.)

How quickly do we do this: run to solutions of our own instead of the One who can solve every problem for us? Before we can even give God a chance to show up, we try to figure it all out on our own.

And when the solutions he offers don't look like what we wanted, we look for different ones—ones that will make us feel more comfortable, in control, and not behind.

But God often provides in unexpected ways. We see this all over Scripture.

He promised Abraham his descendants would be "as numerous as the stars" (Genesis 22:17), but his wife didn't get pregnant until she was *well* past childbearing age (Genesis 21:2).

He had the Israelites march around Jericho for days and then shout so the walls of the city would fall (Joshua 6).

He had David, a young shepherd, use a rock and sling to defeat the giant Goliath and therefore the Philistine army (1 Samuel 17).

He chose Mary, a virgin, to be the mother of Jesus (Luke 1:26-34).

Heck, God spoke through a donkey at one point! (Don't believe me? Look it up for yourself: Numbers 22:21-39.)

But the most unexpected way God provided was in sending his own Son to save us. God sent manna from heaven as to represent to the bread of life he would send from heaven: Jesus.

The manna didn't look like the provision the Israelites wanted.

Just like Jesus didn't look like the Messiah king they were promised.

And if we are honest, God's definition of provision doesn't always look the way we want it to or the way we hope it will. Jesus doesn't seem like enough when I'm trying to navigate moving again. And he definitely doesn't seem like enough when the future feels uncertain and out of my control.

But God's perfect provision for us is promised in Jesus (John 14:6).

Just as God saved his people from Egypt and they still did not trust him, Jesus saves us from sin, and we, too, struggle to trust him—even though saving us from our sin is so much greater than him saving us from temporary circumstances we wish were different.

But we are shortsighted and easily forgetful.

God's perfect provision for us is promised in Jesus.

The Israelites made a massive mess because they were not willing to wait on God's way and timing. After the whole golden calf thing, God kept them in the wilderness another 40 years. They circled around the same mountain over and over, all because they thought their plan was better than God's.

Now, as we discussed in chapter 4, God doesn't withhold things just because we mess up. And as we discussed in chapter 6, God doesn't withhold things just because we want them.

But sometimes he does withhold things because we've made them the *ultimate* thing.

He does not do this because he is arrogant; he does this because he is gracious and after his glory. He knows what's ahead. He knows what's best. He loves us too much to let us find satisfaction in anything that's not him, because everything else will fail us.

At least in my own life, I'm grateful for this truth. I have a pretty active imagination, but even though my dreams are big, God is so much more creative than me. So how much better will it be when he is the one dreaming up how to provide what I need?

What if God's definition of what's good for us is actually better than what we think?

Sometimes God does withhold things because we've made them the *ultimate* thing.

A HARD QUESTION TO ASK OURSELVES

Pastor Tim Keller said it well: "If we look to created things to give us the meaning, hope, and happiness that only God himself can give, it will eventually fail to deliver and break our hearts."[1]

Which is truer than I want to admit.

Every time I put my hope in an outcome or circumstance, I end up heartbroken and disappointed—then I almost always turn around and put the blame on God, as if it's his fault I got let down.

Which makes me wonder: *Do I treat God as just a means to an end?*

Do I really desire what he desires for me, or do I just desire what he can give me?

I will let you take a moment with that thought.

I wish I could say that I desire God more than I desire what I can "get" from him. However, since we are friends now, I will confess to you that I often don't live like that's true. At moments I've wanted to quit God because the hurt from my disappointment felt too great to bear, and I believed the pain was God's fault. (You know, the dangling carrot thing.)

I've watched this happen to others too. When I worked in college ministry, I met a lot of girls who loved God and wanted to grow in their faith. But one by one, I watched a lot of them quit when life stopped going the way they wanted it to.

Some got tired of feeling left out, so they started to party more. Others didn't get the jobs and internships they wanted, so they stopped pursuing their faith. Some chose to marry guys who were not Christians because they didn't want to be single. For one reason or another they slowly decided God was not worth following anymore.

It was hard to watch. It still is.

But the reality is, we all make idols out of the outcomes we want. We may not have given up on God, but turning to created things for happiness is a hard habit to break.

ASSESSING OUR IDOLS

What do we do about all of this? Knowing we can quickly turn what we want into an idol, how do we avoid that?

I want to start by asking ourselves two things:

First, is what we are desiring *actually* good? Think about what we talked about earlier in this chapter. Would the Bible say the outcome or circumstance we are chasing is a good thing? Is it something God says is good, or just something culture says is good? Like a house in a certain neighborhood? Or a particular kind of job?

Second: Will this thing I long for help me or others flourish? So often we will fixate on something we want, but the cost is great to ourselves and others. We become selfish. Here's another example: We don't want good jobs because we are contributing to the flourishing of society; we want them because we can make more money and gain a certain status we think will enhance our lives and make us happier. Same with marriage or children. The Bible says sacrificing for a family will lead to our sanctification, but instead we want them because we want them to satisfy our selfish desires. We have to take a step back and address the motivations behind the "good things" we want.

How can you know if the thing you want has become an idol? Here are some questions to ask yourself:

- Is this a good (biblical) want, or has it become a (selfish) need?
- What am I daydreaming about?
- When I'm quiet in my own mind, where do I find joy?
- How do I spend my money?
- Will what I believe about God change if this desire is never satisfied?
- How will I respond if this prayer is never answered?

- What am I willing to do and/or sacrifice to get what I want?

- Do I believe God is still good if I don't get this? Or is he less good to me if I don't?

- Do I trust God to know if it is better for me to never have this thing I want?

- Am I hoping to get something from this outcome that I can only get from God?

- Am I only looking at what this thing I want gives me and not what I should give to it?

Those are some hard questions to answer because they require us to look at parts of our hearts we'd rather keep hidden. Grace abounds, friend. From the beginning of time, the human heart has been bent to worship the wrong things. But there is hope.

WHEN OUR NEEDS BECOME WANTS

If we are prone to making idols out of good things, then how do we cultivate hearts that want God more than anything else?

We must remember everything God does toward us is an act of love.

This morning in my journal I wrote,

> God, I don't want to question your goodness, I want to draw closer to it. Your goodness is something I should cling to, not question. When I'm questioning you, it's because I feel out of control.

Anything that we put above God forces us to treat God's love as a bad thing. God's love becomes inconvenient because it gets in the way of our idols' success. In 1 Samuel 8, when the Israelites told God they wanted a king so they could be like other nations, God warned them that this would lead to destruction. (And if you keep reading the Old Testament, you'll see that it does!) But the Israelites still chose to reject his love and care toward them because they so badly wanted a physical king to worship instead.

Like the Israelites, we can treat God like he is only good if he aligns with the outcomes and circumstances we want. We question his goodness and get angry at his withholding. Then we become defensive because we perceive his withholding as a loss or failure to our plans.

But his goodness is the common denominator. His goodness is not dependent on our circumstances (Exodus 33:19). If we are questioning his goodness something has changed in *our* faith and in our hearts. His goodness is not dependent on our circumstances.

When our desires are putting demands on God, we are heading in the direction of disappointment.

Instead, we can remind ourselves that God has already given us everything we need. He does not change based on our circumstances. His character remains intact, even if life seems to fall apart.

Then we don't *need* things to go our way, but we are free to want them to.

I think about this when I look back at the ways I've reacted in moments of rejection. In the moments I desperately wanted a relationship, job, or any other small thing to work out, I was devastated when they didn't. But when I remained openhanded and chose to trust God, I felt so much more at peace about things not turning out the way I had hoped.

Yes, we can still be disappointed when things don't happen the way we want them to, but we don't have to be devastated in a way that makes us distrust God and distance ourselves from him.

So, I gently remind myself today: I don't need this relationship to work out to believe God is kind…but I'm free to want it to work out.

I don't need a more long-term living situation to trust God's plan for me, but I'm free to desire it.

What about you? Fill in your own below:

I don't *need* _____, but I'm free to want it.

When our desires are putting demands on God, we are heading in the direction of disappointment.

PRACTICAL WAYS TO FIGHT IDOLATRY

The best way to overcome idolatry is to have a right view of God. We should remind ourselves of how big, powerful, good, and in control he is. When we maintain a perspective of his greatness, we can find comfort in him, rather than idols.

If you're like me, you may want some practical ways to actually do this. And you may be surprised to hear it, but spiritual disciplines can help shape our hearts and desires toward God.

If you've never heard the term *spiritual disciplines*, don't let it scare you. Spiritual disciplines are biblical steps that Christians have intentionally (and sometimes even unintentionally) practiced to orient their lives around God. Several books and resources dive into these practices in detail, but almost all of the books include prayer, reading the Bible, sabbath, silence, solitude, fasting, and feasting as practices. (I've included a glossary and additional resources in the back of the book for reference.)

Making these practices regular in our lives helps us form a right view of God. You don't have to try them all at once. Maybe start with one. As you slowly implement them into your life, pay attention to how the Holy Spirit leads you. You'll start to see your view of God getting bigger, and you'll find more satisfaction in him than anything else.

WHAT I DO KNOW

Okay, so I still don't know how long I'll be living in this basement, nor do I know where this relationship is going. But here's what I do know:

The Lord is with me, and he is for me.

He is not keeping me somewhere he does not want me.

He is not leading me somewhere he has not already been.

What he wants for me is better than what I can understand right now.

The same is true for you.

He is with *you*, right now.

He is for you.

He is not keeping you here unintentionally.

He is not leading you somewhere he has not already been.

What he wants for you is better than what you can comprehend right now.

Maybe if we take a step back and choose patience in the process, we'll see what God has promised. It's not all the things we deeply want, but God himself. Then maybe, just maybe, we'd see that as more than enough.

CHAPTER 8

They Are Not Ahead

AT THE EXACT moment you think you've mastered contentment, comparison creeps in.

For me, it usually starts when I've finished a peaceful time with Jesus in the morning. When I've not only managed to get up early to read my Bible, but I also feel genuinely connected to God. His Word is alive. I literally want to sing shouts of praise. I resolve to start my day thinking, *God is so good, and I'm thankful for the many blessings he has given me!*

After I've said prayers of gratitude and found a positive outlook for the day ahead, I reach for my phone. *I wonder what's happening on social media this morning.* Almost instantly, my mood changes...

I see that a group of my friends got together last night for a beautiful dinner. All smiling and laughing in beautiful dresses and making inside jokes to each other in the comments. And they didn't invite me.

Another friend announces she and her model-looking husband and perfect matching-outfitted children are expecting yet *another* baby.

An influencer I follow has posted from her lavish beach vacation, sporting her perfect sculpted abs in a bikini.

Before I throw my phone across the room with envy, I see

another friend got engaged. Did I mention how massive the ring is?

It takes all of three minutes for my morning of gratitude to get hijacked by jealousy. Discontentment can grow easily when we are distracted by comparison.

At the exact moment you think you've mastered contentment, comparison creeps in.

I know I'm not alone in this. This week I asked my friends on social media if they struggle with comparison, and here are some of the responses:

> "I'm newly married and comparing what we can afford to what other newlyweds have."

> "My job! I feel like everyone else is doing something that gives them more purpose."

> "When I'm trying to be patient about something I'm working toward or praying for."

> "Spiritual maturity. How 'churchy' or 'godly' I am."

> "Career! Am I progressing on the right timeline?"

> "What neighborhood I live in, car I drive, my spouse's career, not having kids."

> "Others have it easier than I do."

> "On Instagram! And when I hear Adele and I are the same age." (This one made me laugh, but also how relatable is it?)

"Body image." (This one was repeated several times.)

"Life milestone timelines (buying a house, engagement, marriage, etc.)."

"Everyone else is put together, and I'm a hot mess."

The items on this list can make us feel behind or not good enough. As if we aren't measuring up.

If we feel behind, that begs the question: What does it mean to be "ahead"? And who gets to decide what "being ahead" means?

We imagine life to be like a straight line. Or like a checklist of things to cross off in a particular order. We've convinced ourselves that life goes up and to the right.

But we've made that up.

Life isn't linear. It ebbs and flows.

Discontentment can grow easily when we are distracted by comparison.

When we see someone who has something we want or is somewhere we want to be, we are tempted to believe some lies. It's easy to think, *I'm never going to get there. Look at how behind them I am. There's a huge gap between where they are and where I am. I'll never achieve what they have achieved.*

Why do we care so much about how we stack up against other people? Would we feel so behind if we didn't have this pattern of comparison?

Trying to define success is difficult because everyone is in process and chasing a moving target. Even if we finally catch up to the people we think are ahead of us, we will always find something else to chase. The person we are looking to as the epitome of where we want to be hasn't "made it." They are in process too.

UNPLUGGING THE SCOREBOARD

Have you ever heard the term *lifestyle creep*? The theory of lifestyle creep suggests that the more money you make, the more money you'll spend. What used to be considered a want or a luxury turns into a necessity. Things you lived without when you made less money become things you can't live without. It's never having enough.[1]

Regardless of your income, factors like your age or relationship status can cause you to feel obligated to live a certain way. We take on external pressures to keep up with others and it becomes a heavier internal pressure than we ever needed to carry.

We get caught up looking at life like a scoreboard, and we try to get as many points as possible. (Look at me using sports analogies! My dad is probably so proud.)

We keep score through accomplishments, achievements, and arriving at certain mile-markers. The more we have in comparison to the person next to us, the more our lives seem to matter. Same for the reverse: The less we have compared to someone else, the less we think we matter.

Then, when someone else "scores," you lose—as if their win equals your loss. We develop a scarcity mentality and assume there's not enough to go around.

But I think it's time to unplug the scoreboard. We have to stop playing the game. It's hard to feel like you are losing when you're not even competing. If we quit striving for what everyone around us has, maybe we would stop feeling behind.

The problem is, we aren't only comparing ourselves to others;

we are also comparing who we are to the version of ourselves we hoped we would be at this point.

You thought you'd be further along in your career by now.

Or have more money in the bank.

Or married.

Or own a house.

Or a certain weight.

Or over a certain struggle.

But you're just not there yet. And you're beginning to wonder if you will ever stop striving to be.

Or maybe you struggle with the reverse: You compare who you are today with a past version of yourself. You wonder if your best days will always be in the rearview mirror.

Depending on the day, I'm either comparing myself to someone else, to an idealized version of myself, or to the person I used to be.

Comparison might be one of the enemy's biggest ploys against us living out who we are called to be in Christ. If he can get us fixated on all the things we are not, we will get stuck there. Instead of running after what God has called us to do, we will run after something else.

> **Comparison might be one of the enemy's biggest ploys against us living out who we are called to be in Christ.**

If we truly let all of that go, I think we would live differently. What would you do if you didn't feel behind?

Would you quit some things? Maybe the job you don't like or find purposeful. Or a relationship you feel obligated to maintain because of the status it brings you. Or that extracurricular activity you do just because everyone around you enjoys it.

Would you try something new? Like the hobby you've always wanted to pick up but didn't think was worth investing in. Or hanging out with people who aren't similar to you or your friends.

Would you follow your passions?

Would you care what people think?

Would you make different decisions?

Be honest: Why are you doing the things you are doing?

Is it because you genuinely want to do them? Or because you think God has called you to them?

Or is it out of pride?

Or fear of failure?

Or because you're comparing yourself to others?

Or due to some cultural expectations you are trying to meet?

I bet we would experience more freedom, more joy, and more satisfaction if we weren't trying so hard to keep up.

One of my favorite verses is Philippians 3:14: "I press on toward the goal to win the prize for which God has called me heavenward in Christ Jesus."

I've saved it as my anthem verse while writing this book, to remind me of what the real prize and reward is. When I am behind on deadlines or I see other people doing things better than me, this verse helps me shift my focus to what matters most—not just in writing this book, but in all of life. I want to be aiming my eyes toward Christ.

If we quit playing the comparison game and instead consider being more like Jesus as our prize, we win.

The ways he has gifted and wired you aren't meant to be compared to the person next to you.

Who God has called you to be is unique.

How God is molding you into that person is also intentional (Psalm 139:13-14).

We have to shift our gaze from what everyone *around* us is doing to what God is doing *in* us.

> # If we quit playing the comparison game and instead consider being more like Jesus as our prize, we win.

GOD IS NOT HOLDING OUT ON YOU

I had a conversation about this with a friend recently. She told me with tears in her eyes how lonely she felt. In her early 30s, she thought life would look a lot different than it did. Her most recent roommate got married and moved out. This was the third roommate of hers to do so.

Circumstantially, she had a lot on her plate—a very sick relative and a packed work schedule, all while trying to make new friends with people who were younger than her and not on the same page. She collapsed into the exhaustion she'd once tried to hide and asked me: "Why does it seem like God makes things easier for everyone else? Everyone around me is coasting along in life getting everything I want. What more does he want from me?"

I sat silently. I had some Band-Aid responses, but I knew they wouldn't help—because I had asked the very same questions.

Friend, I don't know what you wish were different about your life, and I can't claim to have the exact right words to make it better. I am all too familiar with the feeling of life not being fair. But I hope as you read this, you have found a place to feel a little less alone.

I didn't want to offer trite solutions or tidy responses to my friend, and I don't want to offer them to you either. But I do want us to turn to truth.

God isn't withholding something from you. I know that can be really hard to believe. Just because someone else has what you want doesn't mean God doesn't have enough for you. His plans for your life are good, even if they feel anything *but* good right now.

Just look at what Jesus told us: "Why do you worry about clothes? See how the flowers of the field grow. They do not labor or spin. Yet I tell you that not even Solomon in all his splendor was dressed like one of these. If that is how God clothes the grass of the field, which is here today and tomorrow is thrown into the fire, will he not much more clothe you—you of little faith?" (Matthew 6:28-30).

Here is what is true: He has already given you everything. He gave you his Son. His greatest treasure. He gave it all for you. If he was willing to send his only Son to die for you, then he certainly is still working in your life.

Ephesians 2:4-10 shows us this beautifully:

> *Because of his great love for us,* God, who is rich in mercy, *made us alive with Christ even when we were dead in transgressions*—it is *by grace you have been saved.* And God raised us up with Christ and seated us with him in the heavenly realms in Christ Jesus, in order that in the coming ages he might show the *incomparable riches of his grace, expressed in his kindness to us in Christ Jesus.* For it is by grace you have been saved, through faith— and this is not from yourselves, *it is the gift of God*—not by works, so that no one can boast. For we are God's handiwork, created in Christ Jesus to do good works,

which God prepared in advance for us to do (emphasis added).

As hard as it is for us to admit, sometimes Jesus may not seem like enough. We can only see what is in front of us, and Jesus isn't physically in front of us right now—so God feels far from our reality.

God has not forgotten you. If we can somehow believe that, and I mean really believe it, it *would* be enough for us.

This is a daily, moment-by-moment choice. To choose to put our faith in God. To trust his character based on his Word and the ways we've previously seen him moving in our lives. To remind ourselves and each other that his fullness is available to us right now—not one day later on when we have what we want, but today, in the middle of our waiting.

PROVISION COMES IN PACKAGES WE DON'T EXPECT

If you feel guilt or shame about wanting something badly, can I be the one to give you permission to still want that thing you want?

I can say with confidence that God is not sitting up in the sky shaking his head at you because you desire something different for your life (Psalm 51:17). We often project our own fears and insecurities onto God and in the process give him a personality that is not true of him. When I spend time in the Bible, I can see he is not the God I sometimes make him out to be. His true character is marked by kindness, compassion, care, and love.

In the middle of the moments when we think he's shaking his head in judgment and condemnation, I suspect he's doing the opposite. He's looking at you with love. He deeply cares about you and what you want right now. He also knows what's beneath those longings, and he wants to give you what will truly satisfy you.

He's offering you something else, the same thing he always offers: himself and his presence.

God does not withhold his best. He does not give his best to one person and not the other. While what you are facing may feel like the furthest thing from his best, he is not keeping himself from you. He never has, and as long as you are breathing, he is extending the same invitation to draw close to him.

But when I start to question his motives, my own distrust grows. I start to withdraw because I am afraid I cannot really trust his intentions and plans for me. What I think is protecting me is in fact pushing God away.

Yet he patiently pursues me, even as I pull away.

I wonder if his end goal isn't for us to be content, but rather for us to find him. Find him in the things we long for. Find him in the space between where we are and where we want to be. Find that he is not only what we really want, what we actually need. And when we wake up the next day and go looking for contentment and meaning, to find him again.

It reminds me of when Brenna, Shelby, and I found out our first house was being sold. We did *not* want to move. The house was comfortable and easy, and we liked it there. But after the shock wore off, we figured if we couldn't stay, maybe we could at least move somewhere better. If we had to make a change, why not move forward and up?

We got excited and started to dream about where we could go next. A better location? Not a ton of options for three self-employed gals in their midtwenties. More space? Again, we came up short. We looked at so many houses, and our limited options were *worse* than the house we lived in.

At the time, none of our friends could relate. They seemed to be lapping us in life stages, selling their beautifully decorated homes for nicer ones with more space. This left us more frustrated and discouraged by our search. Why did God seem to provide for them but not for us?

Then we moved…to the house next door.

It was almost the same floor plan but with a few differences we didn't love, such as a smaller back porch and one room with ugly purple walls. We got stuck moving 15 feet away, to a house not much different from ours.

Yes, it was provision. But it seemed to represent the season we were all in: wanting to move forward like everyone around us but often feeling like we were moving parallel or backwards.

We spent a rainy December day walking boxes across the yard. Only one of us cried that day, I think, but we were all miserable. Then a package arrived.

We had found this adorable wire lettering company and ordered the word *joy* to hang over the inside of our front door. We wanted that word to define our house because, to be honest, none of us really felt joyful about it.

The package that arrived was much smaller than we had expected, and we realized we had not read the description! We hung the sign right over our light switch because that's how small it was. Immediately we all agreed this was probably a lesson to be learned about joy.

We have to choose to look for it.

Joy is not always big and loud and evident in everyday moments. The sign, meant to remind us of joy, was certainly hard to see some days, and sometimes we didn't even notice it. Usually I was too busy or focusing on other things. But then I'd walk by and the light would catch it just right and remind me that joy is something our Father freely gives us.

While the move was not what we wanted, it was still good. We were given another chance to live together in the same place, but with a new perspective. The Lord had things in store there for each of us. We could all tell you something different we learned about God inside those four walls.

At the time, we saw the move as a lateral move in life. But in hindsight, it was actually a step forward. Not in the ways we thought it would be, or in the ways we wanted it to be, but because of what God wanted to do in each of us. We are all different because of that move.

We discovered something new about God and about ourselves as a result of living in that house. We grew up and learned lessons the hard way. I wonder what we would have missed if we hadn't spent that time there together.

When each of us started to move out, we weren't moving up. I'm not ahead in life because I moved to a new city. Shelby hasn't caught up to everyone else because she got married. Brenna is not behind because she still lives there.

The three of us aren't the same, so it's not worth comparing where we are and where we are going to one another. God has a different plan for each of us, and all of them are good. They are each what is best for us right now. One is not better than the other. They are just different.

HOW WE CAN DAILY COMBAT COMPARISON

In the same way we had to choose to see joy, we also have to choose to not look at other people's lives as markers of what was ahead. We have to look ahead at the right Person: God, who has personally gone before you. Who is leading and guiding us into what's next. When we are so busy looking at what God is doing in other people's lives, we miss what he is doing in ours. We miss what he has already done.

Contentment and comparison cannot coexist.

If contentment is found inwardly, we will not go looking for it externally. Maybe the invitation for us today is to spend time alone with God in his Word. To read the stories of what he has done, and what he will do. To ask the Holy Spirit to examine our hearts and reveal where we've sought to find satisfaction in external things. To allow him to trade our limited, earthly perspectives for hope in his eternal promises.

If contentment is found inwardly, we will not go looking for it externally.

I believe he will do that for you, because I have seen him do it for me.

But what do we do in the meantime? How do we do this *right now*?

I made a list for two reasons: One, because I love lists. And two, because it may be helpful for you to take some simple but practical steps of action to fight off the comparison trap that bombards you every day.

- Take a weekly social media break, even if it's just for 12 hours.
- Set daily time limits on social media apps.
- When you are waiting in line or at an appointment, try paying attention to the people around you instead of looking at your phone.
- Volunteer through your church or a local community organization. Try not to think about your circumstances for a few hours a week.

- Spend 30 minutes outside somewhere. Studies show going on a walk and looking at nature enhances our mental health because it helps us think about something bigger than ourselves.[2]
- Sleep with your phone on the other side of the room. Try not to let it be the first thing you look at when you wake up or the last thing you see before you go to sleep.
- Practice writing a daily gratitude list.
- Find activities you genuinely enjoy doing by yourself.
- Be honest with God and others about the areas where you struggle to feel content.

None of these steps have changed my circumstances, and honestly, they don't always change my feelings. But they do remind me God is not holding out on me.

Friend, our longing for more is a good, eternal desire. When we feel the ache for more, it's a reminder to us that this life isn't it. We are in the "already, but not yet." The world is broken, and eternity has not come. Those desires, whether seemingly big or small, encourage us to lean on the strength that comes from Christ, who gives us everything we need to live fully, right in the middle of our wanting, today.

Contentment looks like being honest about what we want but trusting that God is not withholding his best from us. He gives us the strength to live fully and joyfully where we are, because he has given us Christ.

Satisfaction is not found by looking at what everyone else seems to have. It's found by choosing to look at all God is doing in us.

Everything we could want is found in him. If we can believe that, we can live differently.

CHAPTER 9

They Understand More Than You Think They Do

A FRIEND OF mine was really struggling with all the ways we've talked about feeling behind in life: relationally, financially, and professionally. One day we sat in the white Adirondack chairs on my front porch and talked all about it—the frustration, the questions, the guilt, and the feelings of being stuck. I listened as she unloaded all her thoughts and emotions.

If you haven't figured it out by now, I'm not the friend who tells you what you want to hear. This same friend and I had this conversation a few times, and on this particular day, I wanted to offer a more hopeful perspective. The problem was, she didn't really want to hear it at that moment.

Our lives looked similar at the time, with the exception of one detail: She was two years older than me, so at the time of this conversation, she was 31 and I was 29.

When I tried to offer my encouragement, she snapped at me and said, "You don't get it because you're not in your thirties."

I know this friend didn't mean to be hurtful. She was in a lot of pain, and it may not have been the best time to say what I said. I'm not upset with her response.

That also wasn't the first, or the last, time someone has thrown out the phrase, "You don't get it because (fill in the blank.)"

"You don't get it because you're too young."

"You don't get it because you're not from here."

"You don't get it because you're single."

"You don't get it because you're not a parent."

"You don't get it because you work in ministry, not a corporate job."

Those are just the versions that have been said to me personally. I'm sure you have plenty you could add to the list.

Or some people will say, "You'll understand when..."

"You'll understand when you're older."

"You'll understand when you have kids."

"You'll understand when you're married."

I don't know about you, but I feel immediately discredited in those moments. As if I have nothing to offer because of my circumstances. These words make me question my value in relationships with people whose lives look different from my own.

When that happens, it's easy to want to shut down and shut people out.

WE HAVE TO STOP PUTTING OURSELVES IN DIFFERENT CATEGORIES

We all go through life wondering if we matter. We struggle with feeling behind because we are questioning our worth. We fear we don't add value to our relationships based on our experience (or lack thereof).

So when someone affirms our fears, the walls instantly go up. As a response, we may turn around and do this to other people. We discount their ability to speak into our lives based on their circumstances.

There is a weird juxtaposition of desperately wanting to be understood while at the same time wanting our struggle to be unique.

We want to be able to relate, but we also resist when someone tries to step in to help.

Then we tend to separate ourselves into categories. Just look at churches: couple groups, young adult groups, singles groups, parent groups. We segment ourselves, and then we either feel left out of the groups we aren't in or feel we can't commiserate with those who *are* in our group. Or we assume we need a drastic life change to feel included or to graduate to the "next group."

We miss so much when we get stuck in this cycle.

There's something wonderful about having friends who are in similar situations to you. Commonality and mutual understanding are gifts, and having those types of friendships are important. But there is so much value in having a deep community with people whose lives look different from yours. We all have to stop believing the lie that relatability can only be found when someone is right where we are.

Whether we're comparing ourselves to one another because we don't want to feel inferior, or we're just afraid we don't have a place, we push people away, even when they have a lot to offer us. We deny both them and ourselves a chance to learn something we otherwise wouldn't know.

Don't get me wrong; good, healthy relationships are hard to come by. And trust me, I've been in some unhealthy ones. And some of that unhealthiness came from me. Unrealistic expectations on both sides, lack of boundaries, and immaturity can lead to arguments, misunderstandings, and hurt.

But friendship is worth fighting for. In fact, friendship is biblical. In 1 Corinthians 12:12, Paul gave an illustration of Christians as one body with many parts. Now, he talked about this idea in reference to spiritual gifts, but I think the same principle can be applied to us demographically and socially.

Now if the foot should say, *"Because I am not a hand, I do not belong to the body,"* it would not for that reason stop being part of the body. And if the ear should say, "Because I am not an eye, I do not belong to the body," it would not for that reason stop being part of the body. If the whole body were an eye, where would the sense of hearing be? If the whole body were an ear, where would the sense of smell be? But in fact God has placed the parts in the body, every one of them, just as he wanted them to be. *If they were all one part, where would the body be?* As it is, there are many parts, but one body (1 Corinthians 12:15-20, emphasis added).

In the times we feel left out or like we don't belong, we have to remember that we are all part of a body. Which means, we all have unique contributions to give to one another. We have value to offer in friendship, and that other person does too.

Remember when I told you about my friends Elizabeth, Katie, and Riley? A few years ago, we sat in the corner of a cocktail bar. It was the second time we'd all hung out. All of us were navigating what friendship looked like in our late twenties.

Then Elizabeth did something brave: She asked us if we could commit to being friends. I know this question sounds so elementary, but when you think about it, that's how to start a friendship. She had recently moved to town and didn't know anyone, and she was ready for friendships where she could feel safe and go deeper.

So we just decided right then and there that we were going to be friends. With that we committed to a few things, spoken and unspoken, and it has turned into the sweetest of friendships. And all our lives were a little different because of it, as you read about in chapter 2.

**We all have to stop believing
the lie that relatability can
only be found when someone
is right where we are.**

We are proof that you don't have to be in the same life season as your friends. Married or single, kids or no kids, friendship isn't based on having everything in common. What works about our group is that we don't separate ourselves based on our stages of life. They don't make me feel "lesser" or "behind" because I'm not in their shoes. And I don't make them feel out of touch or insist they can't understand what I am going through.

On top of that, the script flips—often. I'm not the only one who can feel behind in our foursome. For various reasons, we each have our moments of feeling that way; but because we show up each week and choose not to let those feelings of being left out or not enough keep us from deepening our friendships, it works.

Something else that works in our friendship is that we allow one another to step into what we are dealing with, regardless of whether the others "understand." We remember we are all sinners in need of a Savior; we all fall short. None of us has it totally figured out. My pain is not more severe than any of theirs.

Showing up to friendship takes humility. We have to be willing to learn from someone else and admit we don't know everything. We often want to be the experts. Being around people who don't know as much as us shouldn't be what makes us more confident— just as being around people who know more than us shouldn't make us feel insecure. Pride can easily get in the way of building deeper relationships.

Even discipleship is a two-way street. I learn just as much from new believers as I do from seasoned ones. For example, new believers haven't been totally jaded like me. They remind me that what I believe is real and life-changing, which gives me hope. On the other hand, I need people who are older and have been around the block more times than me to teach me too.

Everyone wins when we empathize and seek to understand how the other person feels. It's as simple as saying, "Tell me how this feels for *you*." When we stay curious about how the other person experiences things differently, we can be better friends to one another.

Give each other the freedom to know what's going on in your lives.

Invite one another into the questions you're asking, the wisdom you are seeking, and the problems you are facing.

Everyone wins when we empathize and seek to understand how the other person feels.

Give each other permission and space to speak into each other.

If your friend knows God, then they have the Holy Spirit inside of them—meaning they have the insight and ability to speak into your life. If they know God's Word, they have wisdom to speak truth to you, even if they aren't standing in your shoes.

The same is true on the flip side. It can be tempting to think if we're not in it, we can't speak into it.

The enemy would love for us to believe that. But it's not true.

If we keep reading 1 Corinthians 12, we see the importance of every part of the body:

The eye cannot say to the hand, *"I don't need you!"* And the head cannot say to the feet, "I don't need you!" On the contrary, those parts of the body that seem to be weaker are indispensable, and the parts that we think are less honorable we treat with special honor. And the parts that are unpresentable are treated with special modesty, while our presentable parts need no special treatment. But God has put the body together, giving greater honor to the parts that lacked it, so that there should be no division in the body, but that its parts should have equal concern for each other. *If one part suffers, every part suffers with it; if one part is honored, every part rejoices with it* (1 Corinthians 12:21-26, emphasis added).

THE GIFT OF ASKING FOR HELP

I vividly remember the day after Christmas in 2021, when I flew back to Charlotte after spending Christmas with my family. My throat was starting to feel a little scratchy, but I didn't think too much of it. The changing weather along with cold and flu season were possible culprits, but also traveling is exhausting and wears my immune system down. Of course, this was during the height of the pandemic, and if I so much as felt a sniffle coming on, I chose to avoid people.

Both of my roommates were still out of town, so I went straight home to bed thinking I would sleep off whatever this was.

The next morning, I woke up and felt awful. For the next several days, I stayed on my couch, watched old movies, and binged TV shows. All the while, I tried to not feel sorry for myself.

The only reason I hadn't stayed with my family for the rest of the holidays was because I wanted to celebrate the New Year with my friends. Was that too much to ask? But instead of celebrating together, I was stuck inside alone with no idea how long I would be there. I didn't even have the energy to go outside in the freezing cold and take a walk.

I felt lonelier than I had in a long time.

My roommates were gone, my family was far away, and my other friends were traveling. I didn't have anyone to commiserate with me. And I certainly didn't have a husband or even a boyfriend who (sort of) would have been obligated to help me.

In my pride, I didn't want to ask anyone for help either. Nothing makes me more uncomfortable than asking for what I need. I'd rather solve a problem on my own than know someone is going out of their way because they feel bad for me. A worse scenario: What if I ask for help and they say they no? My stomach hurts just thinking about it.

So instead, I got an Instacart account.

There's nothing inherently wrong with Instacart. In fact, it's a great tool if you hate grocery shopping or don't have time to. But my motivation for getting it was so that I wouldn't have to inconvenience anyone by needing something from them. And part of that was because I didn't think they would understand my need because they all had spouses or family in town who could help them.

When all my friends found out days later that I had been at home sick and ordered groceries in, they were kind of upset with me. They said if they had known, they would have brought me dinner or offered to pick up medicine I needed. I looked back and understood that I hadn't let them be what they are—my friends—when I needed them.

I do this in a thousand different ways a day; I discount my friends' abilities to step into my suffering because I presume they don't understand what I'm dealing with. As a result, I miss out on so much.

THE MOST IMPORTANT THING WE HAVE IN COMMON

Many passages in the Bible are just lists of people's names. I'm guilty of glossing over them because they don't feel applicable to much. But one list I've studied is the one in Romans 16, where Paul wrapped up his letter to the Roman church.

He started by writing about Phoebe, whom he called a *diakonos*, which is the Greek word for a servant, minister, or deacon. She was a key leader in the church of Cenchreae. She was also entrusted by Paul to deliver his letter to Rome and probably had the responsibility of reading the letter out loud on behalf of Paul. He encouraged the Romans to welcome her and publicly honored her for all she was doing to benefit the church (Romans 16:1-2).

About a third of the people Paul listed were women. Which reminds us that women had, and still have, valuable roles to play in building God's kingdom. They were active participants in this community.

In addition to the women, Paul also greeted men, house churches (Priscilla and Aquila's house in Romans 16:3-5), and different households and families (Aristobulus and Narcissus in Romans 16:10-11). He greeted both Jews (Andronicus, Junia, and Herodion) and Gentiles; slaves (Ampliatus, Urbanus, Hermes, Philologus, and Julia); couples (Priscilla and Aquila, Andronicus and Junia); and more. He referred to them as hardworking fellow workers and friends.

What did these different people have in common? *A shared mission to tell the world about Jesus.*

When our communities are centered around sharing the gospel, our differences don't have to divide us. In fact, diversity makes our communities look a lot more like the family of God. And we need gospel-centered community for the church to grow both locally and globally.

As Paul closed this letter, what did he encourage his community to do? Encourage and love one another. And we are called to do the same. Because of Jesus, those who are in Christ are called to love one another as he loves us (John 13:34).

We welcome one another (Romans 15:7).

We confess our sins and pray for one another (James 5:16).

We serve one another in humility (Philippians 2:3).

We live in peace with one another (Romans 12:18).

And as we seek to be a community of believers, we experience more of how Christ loved and gave himself up for us.

When our communities are centered around sharing the gospel, our differences don't have to divide us.

WHERE THE PACE DOESN'T MATTER

I accidentally started a running club this week, which is wildly random. I have no time or business to be in a running club at the moment, but hang with me; I promise we are going somewhere with this.

About a year ago, my friend Shae and I started talking about forming what we called "Slow Girls Running Club." She's run a half-marathon but wouldn't call herself a runner. I ran cross-country my whole life but was (and still am) really out of running shape. For the first time I had to deal with how I could no longer increase mileage and speed as easily as I did in my early twenties.

We wanted an excuse to gather some girls together, and we wanted accountability to run just for the fun of being outside and moving our bodies.

Plus, we both happen to work in marketing, so it was a fun little project to dream about. We didn't actually do anything with the idea for a year. I took the Instagram handle, and we had all the language for marketing written up. We would joke in passing about launching the group one day.

But this week we made a logo and decided to pull the trigger. During our lunch break, we posted on social media with 48 hours' notice for our first running meetup. We also may or may not have made stickers because—let's be honest—we were ready to take this little passion project a little too far.

> *Slow Girls Running Club: where the pace doesn't matter.*
>
> *Who is this for? Girls. Fast girls. Slow girls. Girls who wanna walk and talk. Girls who wanna run their first 5k. Girls who have never run a mile. Moms and strollers. Pregnant mamas. The girlies in progress.*
>
> *Anyone willing to admit life is a marathon, not a sprint.*

I have no idea if it will go anywhere or if we will ever do it again. But a lot of people have responded to it. We both believe there's something to be said for not trying to turn everything into a race—in running *and* in life.

The girls who showed up varied in all aspects of life, as well as running skill and speed. Many of them didn't know each other, and some of them came alone.

But they still showed up. And they ran together.

They started and ended at the same spot, but all took slightly different routes, did varying distances, and ran at different paces.

The goal was not to race. It was just to run.

And I hope they made some friends while they did, one who runs a little faster and one who runs slower. I hope they didn't go in intending to compete, but if they did, I hope they no longer felt the pressure of comparison by the end. I also hope they can call themselves runners regardless of how they finished.

I know it was one random running meetup. However, there's something deeper to notice in it.

All of us desire to belong somewhere. We want to run our races (literally and figuratively), and sometimes we need a little help getting started. We need people who are running too, who will cheer for us and tell us to keep going when we want to quit. People who will notice when we don't show up and remind us our presence matters.

And all of us are beginners in life. It's a good thing to feel the tension of starting, especially in friendship.

So I have a little challenge for you: Pick someone different from who you would typically want to be friends with. Doesn't matter what the difference is—life stage, socioeconomic status, family background, or another church denomination. Then ask them to be your friend. I dare you to try it. You'll be surprised how much that will mean to someone.

Then take a minute to evaluate who you surround yourself with.

Are they calling you to be all God has called you to be, or are they simply justifying where you are?

Are they reminding you what's true, or are you just commiserating over your mutual struggles?

Are you letting their circumstances dictate their ability to speak into your life? Or are you open to learning from a different perspective?

Are you avoiding certain people because their life makes you feel insecure? Or are you only surrounding yourself with people who make you feel better about yourself?

I know some of those questions sting; trust me, I'm stepping on my own toes right now. But I promise you, stretching your friendship muscles is really worth it! Life is so much sweeter alongside people who know and love you no matter where you are.

And friend, you have to go first. If you wait for someone else to, you might wait forever. You have everything you need to bravely take the first step toward being the type of friend you yourself need. I believe in you.

Before we go, here are a few things I've learned that make these kinds of friendships work:

- Make time for each other. Life is busy, but that doesn't mean we can neglect our people. Whether you're scheduling coffee, or weekend games nights, or even running errands, find time to spend together.

- Ask for help, and show up to help them even when they don't ask. This is the hardest for me, but being honest about what we need allows everyone to feel safe and cared for.

- Ask for accountability, and hold each other accountable. This doesn't have to be as scary and complicated as we make it. It's as simple as one person saying, "Can you ask me about this later?" and the other person doing so.

- Don't take everything so personally, and believe the best in one another. Remain humble.

- Have fun! Plan the trips. Throw the parties. Celebrate all the milestones. Not everything has to be deep conversations about life and faith. You can just enjoy each other's company.

We're about to talk a lot more about that last point in the next chapter.

I know this may sound like work, but I promise it's so worth it! We don't have to wait for the friendships we want. We can go out and make them. And when we do, we build communities where everyone, regardless of age or life stage, can have a place to be valued and belong.

CHAPTER 10

An Obvious (but Unlikely) Way to Love Your Life

IT CAN BE challenging to celebrate someone who has what we want—especially when it feels like we have nothing to celebrate for ourselves.

Another baby shower invitation showed up in my mailbox. Don't get me wrong, I love my friends, and I *love* their babies. But I have already either thrown or attended seven other showers in the previous few months, and both my heart and my bank account are running low on celebratory energy.

Then, this morning, I sat and listened while one friend complained about a wedding she was in and how tired she was of all the festivities. The other friends with us chimed in and agreed. Our calendars were full, and we wished we could say no to some of these events.

Meanwhile, I timidly texted some friends about getting together for my birthday. I worried they wouldn't want to come because they were too busy or because my birthday wasn't as important as the other things they had going on.

But before I had too much time to question my invitation, another friend got a massive promotion and the group chat blew up with plans to go to dinner and celebrate. To be honest, cheering this friend on felt harder than I wanted it to. Recently, I have been having several hard conversations with my boss about what upward mobility at my job could look like, and things aren't going the way I'd hoped.

But even though celebrating can sometimes feel like a burden, choosing to celebrate others and ourselves is one of the best ways to overcome the cynicism we feel toward our circumstances.

When you think about it, celebration is a huge cadence of our lives and calendars. We mark holidays, anniversaries, birthdays, and seasons. In fact, it's biblical to celebrate. The word *celebrate* is translated from the Hebrew verb *hagag*, which means "to prepare, keep, or observe a feast or festival."[1] Scripture outlines so many feasts and festivals: the Passover, the Festival of Harvest, the Festival of Tabernacles, and more. The reason for celebration was to remember what God had done for his people.

> ## Choosing to celebrate others and ourselves is one of the best ways to overcome the cynicism we feel toward our circumstances.

We should celebrate today for the same reason: to remember and rejoice in what God has done. It doesn't always have to look like a party or an event, but celebration helps you invite others to acknowledge a moment that matters, a moment you don't want to forget.

We often find ourselves busy attending celebrations of other people's weddings, babies, promotions, and houses. And these milestones are worth celebrating! But they are not the only things in life we should honor and acknowledge.

We can be tempted to downplay our own achievements and milestones because they look different from those of our friends. As a result, our lack of celebrating can create feelings of behindness that we weren't meant to feel.

When we refuse to celebrate what's going on in our lives because the successes don't seem as significant as what others are celebrating, we discount where God has us right now.

We can't keep looking ahead at future possibilities to rejoice. Those will come, but we don't want to look back and regret not taking a moment to savor the goodness of right now.

CELEBRATE SIMPLY SHOWING UP

A few friends and I have a group chat called "The Get It Done Girlies."

The sole purpose of this group chat is to text each other photos of when we workout. There are no goals. No trying to hit a certain number of times per week. No one is training for a race or trying to run fast. We all know the value of moving our bodies. Not because we need to look a certain way or achieve a standard, but because it makes us feel better.

Whether we take a short walk or a boot camp class, we text a selfie and the others cheer. There's no pressure or shame to do it every day. On the days we don't have time or want to take a day off, we're still cheering for the others in the group who moved that day without comparing.

It's not about milestones; it's about celebrating the daily moments we show up for ourselves.

But that is the beauty of it. We're not waiting for the day we accomplish something great; we are enjoying our small day-to-day wins.

We have to get good at letting ourselves be celebrated in order to celebrate others. When we are constantly building others up but don't allow them to reciprocate, we can start to feel less-than or bitter. Think about it: We are all a little awkwardly bad at receiving compliments. We don't know how to let others pour into us—which is sort of sad to think about!

Celebrating the big and small things feels like a way to see people and be seen.

Celebration invites intimacy and requires vulnerability. To tell someone you're working toward specific goals or achievements demands vulnerability because there's always the possibility of things not working out. But it's even more beautiful to achieve that goal with a community cheering you on. This community gets to pray for you as you work toward a goal, and then they get to rally around you when you experience a win. On the flip side of that, when you face setbacks or even failures, you're able to grieve these losses within the safety of a community that shares your pain. These people get to love and stand by you when something doesn't turn out the way you'd hoped.

Celebration invites intimacy and requires vulnerability.

This is also how we can breathe life into our friendships. We can remind our friends they are not the sum total of their circumstances—that even the smallest of their wins is worth celebrating.

Start asking your friends how you can be excited for them.

Why does this feel so difficult to do?

One reason may be because we have a hard time living in the moment. We're so quick to move on to the next thing despite having just arrived at the first thing. This is why, for example, the second we start dating someone, people start asking when we're getting married. Or the day you get back from your honeymoon and everyone's suddenly interested in when you're having a kid. (Which is so awkward to talk about...They know how babies are made, right?!) The moment you have a baby, people want to know when you are having the next one.

Or they ask, "Do you love your job? Do you think you'll be there awhile? Are you planning to stay in your house or do you want to get a bigger one in a nicer neighborhood?"

For example, I've been dating someone long-distance for six months, and daily I get asked, "Is it serious? Which one of you is going to move? Do y'all talk about getting married?"

When I moved into my new place two weeks ago (remember the basement?), people started asking how long I'll be here, where I'm going next, and if I'm going to move to the city my where boyfriend lives.

And I found myself wanting to scream, *"I just got here! Can I have a moment, please?"*

Or, *"If I knew the answers to those questions, I probably wouldn't be here right now!"*

(Clearly I needed to let that frustration out...)

People are usually well-meaning when they ask these questions. But by adding to the pressure we are already feeling, these questions compel us to look constantly ahead, always moving toward bigger life changes or events on our calendar.

And we are missing what is happening right now, right here.

Even in our day-to-day conversations with others, we get caught up in talking about what's next or what sort of big news there is to share.

Think about it: How often do you get asked the question, "What's new?" when you're catching up with a friend you haven't seen in a week or maybe even months? Then suddenly you're forced to reflect on what's changed since you last talked.

The dread begins to fill you. You realize not only is nothing new, but also nothing you hoped to be new has happened either. The spiral starts as you wonder: *Does everyone except me have something new going on?*

If you haven't gone on a trip, started dating someone, gotten pregnant, or been given a promotion, this question can be paralyzing. It makes me wonder if my life is boring. But what if everyone else feels this way too?

Can we stop measuring whether life is noteworthy or worth celebrating based on these things?

The reality is that most of our minutes are spent in the mundane. More than that: I think God offers abundance in the day-to-day, nothing-exciting-or-new moments of our life. Why else would we spend most of our time there? We can easily miss God's presence when we aren't being present.

Just read any of the Gospels and you'll see that Jesus spent most of his time walking, sleeping, eating, drinking, spending time with his friends, spending time alone with God, and doing his ministry job. None of that was glamorous, it was just what was in front of him each day. He knew what was ahead: suffering on the cross, a beautiful resurrection, and bringing his kingdom to earth. (You know, the actual big and grand things.) Yet he was faithful with what was in front of him in the meantime.

Jesus changed the world by simply living out his calling in his places, with his people. And you and I are called to do the same.

When we find ourselves aching for the next trip, for a relationship status to change, or for something in our lives to seem Instagram-worthy, I want us to remember:

The minutes spent in the mundane make up our lives. Let's not miss them.

We can easily miss God's presence when we aren't being present.

I've put together 30 questions that are better than "What's new?" to ask someone the next time you're hanging out with them. You can find them on page 207. These questions will make the other person feel seen, loved, and valued for who they are, not what they have going on. I've used them personally and can vouch that they do help deepen friendships.

A MUSCLE WORTH BUILDING

Even as I write today, I want to be in a celebratory mood. I could write a list of reasons to be, and yet, I've had a hard time with this chapter. Which reminds me: The ability to celebrate is a discipline we have to fight for.

Psalm 27:13 says, "I remain confident of this: I will see the goodness of the LORD in the land of the living."

That verse reminds me why building the muscle of celebration matters. We need to look for the goodness of the Lord today and help others do the same.

One way I'm developing this discipline is by remembering dates to celebrate people. Whether the anniversary of their job, the day they brought home their puppy, or another life event, I put the date in my calendar so I don't forget to acknowledge it.

This technique for keeping track has been especially crucial for acknowledging not just moments of happiness, but also moments of grief—such as the day my friend lost a parent, or the day another friend suffered a miscarriage. It may feel like those aren't things to *celebrate*, but celebrating is about remembering; it's about honoring. Telling someone you remember their pain makes them feel less alone. Whether it's acknowledging they made it through the hard things, or simply telling someone you haven't forgotten, those are both ways we can be there for someone.

My friend plants flowers on the anniversary of her dad's death every year. Then her siblings all go to his favorite breakfast spot to exchange memories and stories and laugh.

Remembering can be healing.

Find tangible ways to show up and celebrate someone. It can be as simple as saving someone's coffee order in their contact information on your phone. Then the next time you have a moment to honor them, you can surprise them with their favorite drink.

Learn to celebrate where you are too. If you were there, then you wouldn't be here.

A celebration doesn't have to be a party. It can be making dinner plans the day you get your hair done so you can show it off. Or making a registry for house (or apartment) stuff you can share with friends when they ask you what you want for your birthday. It can be inviting friends over to celebrate finishing that one project that's been consuming your life for months.

I personally don't think you can ever be "too much" when it comes to this. In a world that tries to downplay everyday things, why not just be excited? Go big! Celebrating produces so much joy. It's a great way to stop manipulating your hope.

Every win is worth the hype. Make it a big deal!

AN EXERCISE FOR REMEMBERING

Time tends to slip away when we don't take a moment to reflect on all that has happened. But we don't always have to rely on other people to mark moments of importance. We can celebrate on our own too.

I worry we miss the best parts of life because we are so busy moving on to the next one.

One of the ways I practice slowing down is by taking a moment to write down the small moments I want to remember.

What if you took a few minutes today to just reflect on the past month? Grab a journal or open a note on your phone. Maybe turn on your favorite album. Pick up a fun beverage from your most-loved coffee shop. Write about the highlights of this month and how God was there.

Here are some reflection questions to ask yourself:

1. What was good this past month?

2. How did I show up to my life?

3. Where did I see God move?

4. What am I hopeful for next month?

I'll share my answers with you too:

1. Some good things for me: celebrating in all the ways— bridal showers and baptisms, thirtieth birthdays and first birthdays, engagements and babies and even some bittersweet see-you-laters.

2. I showed up at work. I showed up for my people when they needed me and for my quiet time even though it looks different in this season. And for my body by getting out of my comfort zone to join a new gym and start running again.

3. God moved in small, seemingly insignificant ways. I so wanted him to move in big ways. To speak clearly or to answer prayers. But instead, he just reminded me he's always moving. I see it in the way the light shines on my desk at work. Or in a refreshing conversation with

a friend. In the changes I didn't ask for, nor did I really want. He moved, but he stayed the same, and somehow that is all I needed this month.

4. I'm hopeful what's ahead will be full of the same small, beautiful moments and that the Lord will draw my attention to them.

Many of the stories and moments I've shared with you in these pages are documented in a journal somewhere. As I've worked on this book, I've gone back and looked at them. Like looking at old pictures, reading those journals reminds me of the best memories. I've found prayers I forgot I prayed that are now answered. Each time I sit down to reflect on these questions, I leave a little more hopeful and a lot more grateful for the life God has given me.

IT'S NOT ABOUT THE PARTY, BUT WHAT THE PARTY REPRESENTS

Back to the birthday party invitation I sent out. The celebration was nothing big or flashy; my friends and I met at a brewery on a Tuesday night. My roommates and I snagged a table, and within 20 minutes, we had to push a few more together.

It wasn't even a milestone birthday. I didn't *need* to celebrate it. But my friends showed up with their dogs, husbands, and babies. In their work clothes and workout clothes. Some of them knew each other, and others didn't. Friends from church, work, my neighborhood, and even the gym.

I looked around and realized how the people around me had been strangers a few years ago. Then I thought about all the ways—big and small—we've shown up to celebrate each other since then. The get-together wasn't so much about me as much as it was about the life we'd lived together over the past year.

I wanted to bottle up that moment and keep it forever because it didn't feel like a party to mark another year of my life; it felt like a snapshot of what God had been building for years.

I told everyone that all I wanted for my birthday was to get one group picture. I never wanted to forget that I had moved to a city where I didn't know anyone, but two years later, a group of people had gathered together because I invited them.

That picture has been my laptop background for the last year while I've written this book. It reminds me that celebrating and showing up are worth it. In the moments I feel alone, sitting at my computer and typing away, I can look at the snapshot and quickly remember that I'm not alone. Everyone in that group of people has sent me texts, bought me coffees, and invited me to dinner throughout this process. Before they've read a word of this book, they've cheered me on. They didn't wait until it was done and out in the world to show me they were proud of me.

Which is the exact kind of friend I strive to be to them.

Before this chapter ends, I want to tell you about my friend Anna Lee because she is better at celebrating than anyone I know. She never plans just a casual get-together; it's always a full-on event! Regardless of the occasion—the twenty-first night of September, the anniversary of someone moving to Charlotte, or a new haircut—she goes big. She does not shy away from sharing what she's excited about in her life, or from making you more excited for what's going on in yours.

She also has experienced more pain than anyone in their mid-twenties should have, which makes her joyfulness even more inspiring. So, as I finished this chapter, I asked her, "Why is life worth celebrating?" And she gave me the best answer:

I want to be an active participant in this one precious, beautiful life God has gifted me with. God doesn't ask us to sit on the sidelines. He invites us to participate. On earth as it is in heaven.

I couldn't have said it any better.
Let's rejoice. On earth as it is in heaven.

CHAPTER 11

When the Thing You Looked Forward to the Most Made You Feel the Worst About Yourself

JUNE 2023

I'm calling myself a "hope failure" this week—which I'm not sure is even a thing, but it describes how I feel. Doubt and fear are loud in my mind and heart, and I'm having a hard time not listening to them. There's a particular situation I really hope works out. But whether it does is completely out of my control.

I want to feel like I've made progress in this area. To be able to say I know with confidence God is who he says he is and will do what he says he's going to do. To firmly believe that just because I can't see him, doesn't mean he's not there. But right now, I *struggle* to believe that is true.

Today I'm fearful of what's ahead, so I want to run harder and get in front of it. I find myself wanting to beat what I'm afraid of to the punch—believing that if I just try a little harder, I can save myself from getting hurt.

Which is an illusion at best.

I'm not trusting God to look out for me. In fact, I'm not trusting his character at all. Once again, I feel like he is dangling a carrot in front of me, just out of reach. And I worry he has no intention of ever giving it to me—which does not, in any way shape or form, feel like kindness. It actually just feels cruel.

I know I'll survive if this situation doesn't work out. But I am far past the point of being disappointed if it doesn't; if that happens, I know I will be devastated. And I hate that I've let myself become so vulnerable.

I find myself retracing my steps and wondering if I missed something. Did I not hear God on this? Did I do this to myself?

Those old ways of thinking can creep back in so quickly.

I said I wasn't going to manipulate my hope. I said I was going to let myself be excited. That I wasn't going to let potential future sadness steal from happiness I can experience today.

But right now, that feels terribly risky. I want to go back to the point when I wasn't at risk of getting hurt, making a mistake, or letting anyone else down.

I wonder if hope ever gets easier. I don't want anxiety to drive my actions or emotions because these anxious thoughts are telling me lies, and I know the fear I feel is temporary.

The enemy wants to steal, kill, and destroy everything that is good (John 10:10). Sometimes he uses fear and anxiety to do that. If he can keep us believing lies, we will have a hard time stepping out in faith and obedience. He wants us to play it small and safe, so he will try to scare us with worst-case scenario thinking. But I don't want to let him win. If what I'm facing today doesn't work out, I don't want it to be because the enemy got to me with fear. I want it to be because it was not God's best for me.

Which can feel tricky to determine, but it is possible.

WHEN OUR FEELINGS LIE TO US

How do we tell the difference between the enemy and our emotions?

Feelings aren't necessarily truth you can trust, but they do factor in how you relate to God. As Lysa TerKeurst says, "Feelings are indicators, not dictators."[1]

Part of embracing and thriving where we are is recognizing the emotions that come with not being where we thought we would be. It's okay to have feelings, but they shouldn't make all our decisions for us.

I often beat myself up for not being more grateful and content. But in an effort to avoid confronting difficult feelings, I shove them down and put a Bible verse over them. Or I lie to myself about how I actually feel. In the long run, that doesn't help anything.

Do you ever feel this way?

While my life right now is full of wonderful things, life also feels hard. Balance seems impossible to find amid a schedule with no margin and constant changes. The routines I usually cling to aren't helping in this season.

And I feel guilty for saying that because in many ways, I'm living out what I've prayed for. When someone asks how I'm doing, I enthusiastically say, "Life is great! I am doing good. Things just feel kind of crazy and out of control." And both can be true at the same time.

Because even when we get the things we begged God for, the reality is those things will never satisfy us. We can desire something so deeply, but when it finally comes, we still end up disappointed. Then we can try too hard to hang on to it. Fearing what will happen if we lose it, we get anxious and try to take control. Then our anxiety spirals out of control.

I'm seeing this play out in one particular relationship in my life. For most of my late twenties, I wanted to be dating someone. I dreamt about having someone to call after work, to have baked-in plans with for Friday nights. After years of praying, going on bad first dates, and getting my hopes up only to be disappointed by date number three, I started dating a guy I had known for years.

The third date came and went, and things were still going well. Before we knew it, we were traveling back and forth every couple of weeks in a long-distance relationship.

We can desire something so deeply, but when it finally comes, we still end up disappointed.

We got serious quickly. I think we both thought, *This is it.* But the past week was exhausting. Between getting sick and moving, I had nothing to give. I felt emotionally drained.

Traveling back and forth was a *lot.* Trying to communicate about hard things over FaceTime and phone calls took a toll. It was hard to be in different places, and sad every time we had to say goodbye. But at that time, there weren't any solutions to fix these hurts. It was too soon for one of us to consider moving, but neither of us wanted to break up either.

The things that were hard for us weren't out of the norm for a dating relationship. Put any two sinful people together, and you are guaranteed some conflict. But I started to freak out.

In my fear of being too much for him emotionally, my anxiety spiraled. Because I so desperately didn't want to lose him, I started trying to control his perception of me. I stuffed down my emotions all day, but when I lay awake at night, I was left with the aftermath of it all: the fear, the worry, the overwhelm.

Which is what happens when we don't trust God.

It's normal to feel most anxious when we fear losing what we most love.

And if we are honest, what we most love is often not God.

And while I know he will not tolerate any idols I put above him, he is not some cruel, cosmic cop waiting to punish me by taking that valuable thing away from me.

I know people who idolized marriage and still got married.

Who were obsessed with their career and moved up the promotion ladder.

Who wanted fame and recognition more than anything else in the world and achieved it.

I also know people who trusted in God yet never seemed to get *anything* they wanted. And a few of them are the happiest and most content people I've ever met because they know something I have long tried to grasp: God is enough.

We have to be okay without *that thing*.

Without the relationship.

Without the money.

Without the desired outcome.

Not because our desires don't matter to God, but because he alone has to be enough to satisfy us.

WHERE WE TRIP OVER THIS

On occasion I will remember that God really is all I need. Usually when I'm in the middle of worship. Or sitting still in my corner chair reading my Bible in the morning. In these moments, I'm utterly convinced all the things we've talked about in the book are true, and I'm ready to live them out.

Then, before the end of the day, something hijacks that peace, and I'm right back to feeling behind again.

You know the feeling when you're driving home from a girls' night and suddenly find yourself trying not to burst into tears.

Because even though you were so looking forward to spending time with your friends, it somehow made you feel worse about yourself.

Maybe you wore the wrong outfit. You did not get the dress code memo, and everyone else showed up cute and completely put together. They all seem to know what's trendy, but you clearly do not. Then you realize you have nothing new to share, even though everyone else seems to be crushing it at life: new boyfriends, new cars, new promotions.

You overhear a few of them talking about something they are doing together next week, and you realize you aren't included. You wonder if you did something wrong, or maybe you're just not cool enough. You've never felt more alone.

All of a sudden, what you wore to the outing has turned into you questioning if you are ruining your entire life...

Or for my male readers, maybe you're spending a weekend afternoon on the golf course. You're pumped for some time with the guys after a long week. You're feeling pretty good about yourself—you went the extra mile at work and managed to go to the gym for a few days in a row. You even attended that prework Bible study that is often hard to make.

While you're warming up, one guy is talking about a massive deal he closed. Another is up for promotion and buying yet another house. This one is even bigger and in a better location. Then one of them starts telling you about the extravagant European vacation he's taking with his wife for their anniversary.

Now you're riding in the cart, silently questioning yourself. You start to withdraw, and you're not even playing that great. Now you're wondering, *What's the point of trying?* At this rate, you'll never be as successful or well-respected as these guys, no matter how hard you try.

Maybe this spiral plays out a little differently for you, but we can all slide down the slope in our heads when we worry we aren't measuring up.

We want the trip, the event, the relationship, or the success to fix us. But none of those can fix us because they aren't Jesus. The things we achieve can temporarily satisfy us, but when our excitement fades or our circumstances change, we're left with an even bigger pit of longing because our dreams failed to meet our expectations. Now we feel even more empty and hopeless.

But what Jesus offers will actually fix us: salvation and grace.

Grace and salvation are not achievements to earn or prizes to compete for. They are gifts freely given to us:

> Praise be to the God and Father of our Lord Jesus Christ, who has blessed us in the heavenly realms with every spiritual blessing in Christ. For he chose us in him before the creation of the world to be holy and blameless in his sight. In love he predestined us for adoption to sonship through Jesus Christ, in accordance with his pleasure and will—to the praise of his glorious grace, which he has freely given us in the One he loves. In him we have redemption through his blood, the forgiveness of sins, in accordance with the riches of God's grace that he lavished on us. With all wisdom and understanding, he made known to us the mystery of his will according to his good pleasure, which he purposed in Christ, to be put into effect when the times reach their fulfillment—to bring unity to all things in heaven and on earth under Christ (Ephesians 1:3-10).

Who else can give us a new family?
Who else can give redemption?
Who else can forgive our sins?
Who else gives us eternal life?
No one but Christ alone.

Jesus is the best news of all. He gives us the freedom to let go of our disappointment when the things we want end up making us feel worse about ourselves. We don't have to put hope or weight in them. We can enjoy them without expecting them to solve all our problems.

How do we receive these free gifts? I'll say it again: If you haven't surrendered your life to Jesus, see "How to Know Jesus Personally" on page 199. It is the most important takeaway in this book.

I also love what Colossians 1:16-17 says: "In him all things were created: things in heaven and on earth, visible and invisible, whether thrones or powers or rulers or authorities; all things have been created through him and for him. He is before all things, and in him all things hold together."

God created all things, and he holds everything together.

God alone can truly satisfy us.

God is also before all things, which means he is never behind (Revelation 22:13).

INTERRUPTING THE LIES IN YOUR HEAD

We can apply all the principles in this book, but we will still inevitably have anxious moments that can send us right back to questioning if we really are where need to be. When that happens, we can feel so defeated. As if we haven't made any progress at all.

> ## God is also before all things, which means he is never behind.

The words we say to and about ourselves matter, which is why knowing the truth of God's Word and is crucial. Colossians 3:16

says, "Let the message of Christ dwell among you richly." When we spend time meditating on and memorizing what the Bible says is true, we are better able to recognize and fight the lies in our heads. Ephesians 6:17 calls God's Word a sword to be used as a weapon against the schemes of the enemy.

Romans 12:2 says we are transformed by the renewing of our minds. That means we can replace those fears and lies with the truth of what God's Word says. But we have to actually know what God's Word says in order to do that.

My pastor in college once said, "Whatever you meditate on, you magnify; and whatever you magnify, you let it control you." It's easy to let our minds get caught in a loop if we meditate on negative thoughts. When that happens, those thoughts can become bigger than they need to be and then we can start making poor decisions. But when we flip that on its head and are able to interrupt those thoughts with God's truth, we make him bigger and then don't respond out of heightened emotions.

Now when I sense the spiral coming on, I practice pausing and remembering what's true. I even wrote a little script to say out loud that you can borrow:

> I am not behind. I am still moving forward and making progress. Even when my life doesn't seem interesting, God is still intentionally writing my story. Even when I'm not included, God still invites me in. Even when I feel inferior, my identity does not change. God has not left me here. He is with me and is working out the details even when I can't see them. And because of that, I am more than okay. I am exactly where God wants me. Lord, please help me to love it here.

Sometimes before hanging out with a group of people, I will repeat these words to myself. I also keep the words in a note on my phone to read before driving home. And when I need them, I also have several verses memorized that I repeat over myself.

Feel free to switch out some of the phrases to fit your situation, or choose a verse that applies to your circumstances. The point is to remind yourself what is true when a situation or your feelings are saying otherwise.

YOU DON'T HAVE TO BE ENOUGH

February 2023

After one of my first visits to see the guy who would later become my boyfriend, Madi picked me up from the airport. She knew from experience how hard it is to come back from a long-distance visit, so she pulled up with her windows rolled down, blasting "Love on the Weekend" by John Mayer to try to diffuse my sadness.

As we started driving, she turned down the music, looked me dead in the eye, and said, "Are you moving?"

While nothing had been discussed or decided then, my heart kind of stopped because part of me thought I might. However, I told her the honest truth: I didn't know. It was way too soon to say for sure.

Madi isn't usually one to make sweeping statements or assumptions, but she said something then that struck me: "Meghan, I think you've accomplished everything you came to Charlotte to do."

I didn't know how to respond. Surely that wasn't true. At this point, I'd only been in Charlotte for three-and-a-half years. I'd finally gotten my footing—wasn't this when I'd finally get to enjoy the good part? All the years of work to establish a community and a life I loved had started to pay off.

Plus, I wasn't totally sure what I'd come to Charlotte to accomplish.

When I first showed up, I had a U-Haul full of my earthly possessions and no clue what was ahead. I'd simply moved because I'd gotten a job and thought it would be the best next step in life. I couldn't have imagined this place ever feeling like home…and I certainly didn't expect it to be a permanent move.

For the first couple of years, I'd cried every time I left my hometown because that was the only place that made me feel safe and secure. (I'd also moved right before the world literally imploded from COVID-19.) Being so far from the people and places that were comfortable and familiar during those years had been scary.

But she pointed out that I'd still done it.

I'd moved to a city where I didn't know anyone.

I'd created a home and built a community.

I'd taken on the job and then worked hard to get a book deal.

Fast-forward to now, a few months after she picked me up from the airport. And I still haven't stopped thinking about what she said.

What do her words mean for my future here?

At community group last night, my friend Lindsay asked me how I was doing. The women in our group have walked closely with me through these months, but as we sat around a fire, she asked, "How are you feeling about the whole untethered thing? You haven't brought it up in a while, so I wondered if something had changed."

And I realized: The untethered feeling is gone.

What did change?

Today, Charlotte feels more like home than my hometown. In fact, I'm struggling to remember the last time I cried about leaving the beach. It's been at least a year. But it's not because Charlotte feels like the safest and most secure place I could be.

I think it's because for the first time, I feel safe and secure within myself.

And not just within myself, but with God.

For years, I've longed for a sense of home, to feel settled where I am and in who I am. The move to Charlotte stripped away the crutches I'd been leaning on: being close to family, feeling familiar with where I lived, being known by a lot of people. I leaned on those things for security, and even leaned on those people more than I leaned on God. I may have even relied on the faith of others to keep me going—which I now know was not sustainable.

I spent a lot of time trying to catch up after I moved. To build a life here. In some ways, this was good. Putting effort into making friends and finding a sense of belonging served me well. In other ways, I exhausted myself. But overall, God was faithful to me in moving. Even when I questioned whether he was present with me. Even when I was less than faithful to him.

I had a moment last summer when I decided to stop trying to catch up. I was done trying to be anyone other than myself. Coming off the heels of what seemed like a big rejection, I knew I had to make a choice: I could sulk in my disappointment or keep doing what God had put in front of me. So I chose to follow him.

To tell the truth, it wasn't even a spiritual choice. I didn't pray about it or ask God what he thought. I didn't seem to have another option. I could keep following the God I said I believed in, or I could quit trying so hard to be who I thought God expected me to be.

Quitting sounded appealing, if I'm honest, but I knew it would make an even bigger mess of my heart and my life. Instead, I decided to stop caring so much about everything.

Maybe that sounds strange. It wasn't that I no longer cared

about God, or about living in a way that honored him. I think I need to stop feeling like his soldier and start feeling like his daughter again.

Working in ministry has been such a gift, but I can see how doing so has also tricked me into thinking the only way to please God is to work *for* him. When really, he's also asking me to work *with* him (Matthew 11:30). And there is a big difference in those positions!

A soldier is performing a duty. A child lives from a place of delight.

I had come to care so much about earning God's love that I had forgotten how to simply experience it.

Maybe that's where you find yourself too: hustling and out of breath from trying to be enough when God never asked you to be. The world will tell you to try hard, do more, and look good while doing it. But your Father is not putting that pressure on you.

IT ALL COMES BACK TO SURRENDER

I used to think this newfound settledness came because I turned 30. I'm aware there's nothing magical about an age, but as you already know, I'd spent a lot of time bracing myself for that birthday. Even though exiting my twenties looked nothing like I thought it would, I had made peace with entering a new decade.

So I figured maybe this contentment came from choosing to move on.

But now, as I am writing, I think it's deeper than that.

All the wrestling, the moving, the transitions, the changes, and the trying to catch up wore me down. I couldn't put my finger on it before now, but perhaps my struggling brought me to a deeper level of surrender. I was too tired to keep fighting for the life I thought I wanted. In a way, I gave up.

I gave up on creating an idealized version of myself.

I gave up on some ideas of what I thought would make me happier.

I gave up on striving so dang hard.

And in giving those things up, I found a few surprises along the way.

I found hope again. After years of assuming God was going to let me down, I found hope in him, what he was doing in me, and his plans for my life.

I found a quiet confidence in who I am. In the ways God specifically made me and gifted me.

I found joy. In enjoying life again and not taking everything so seriously.

I found home. With just him and me.

In some ways, I found God again. Not God as I'd created him to be. Not One who is distant or leading me on. Not One who constantly disappoints me.

But One who is actively close and present with me.

We did it. God and I. Well, mostly God, but I was there too. We built a life I love, even though I still don't have everything I want. In fact, some of the things I had when I started this book aren't here anymore—while other things I've wanted for so long seem to be entering the picture.

I'm still afraid to get my hopes up. I know the feeling of being let down all too well, and I don't want to experience it again.

And now I know that regardless of what lies ahead, that assurance in God isn't going away.

If I stay in Charlotte for a few more months or a few more decades, it doesn't really matter because wherever I go next, I know God has me. He is with me. He's not leaving me. My home is found in him. Not in a place, a person, a circumstance, or anything else.

I can stand on my own two feet, just me and God. Completely tethered in his love and care for me.

I wonder if the whole reason I moved was to learn that. And if that's the case, it was more than worth it.

CHAPTER 12

This Isn't What It's All About

JUNE 2023

At this moment, I really want the things that make me feel behind.

I want to be married.

I want my own house.

I want a new workout outfit from lululemon.

I want a car from this decade.

And if I'm honest, today I want all of it more than I want God.

The idealized version of the life I desire sounds so much better than the one God has granted me at the moment. I don't want to pour my guts and heart out on these pages; I'd rather be at the beach enjoying an ice-cold beverage and not thinking about anything at all.

But deep down, I also know I want more than that.

Jesus feels far away some days. Real life is happening, and he seems distant from that reality. I haven't forgotten what he accomplished by dying on the cross; but my life is crowding in. There are things to do, bills to pay, people to deal with.

Then something interrupts the day in and day out: The truth of what Jesus did and what we're called to do is a whole lot louder than I can possibly ignore.

For just a moment, everything in life feels so temporary.

An influential Christian leader went to be with Jesus recently. Pastor Tim Keller's life and legacy will likely be talked about for generations to come. His books and sermons shaped me and so many people whose faith I admire and look up to greatly.

But I was shocked by how much I cried on the day he died.

I knew through social media that he had battled cancer for years, but I didn't follow updates closely. To me, when his family posted he was giving up the fight, the end seemed sudden. On that day Michael, his son, posted on Instagram:

> In prayer, he [Tim Keller] said two nights ago, "I'm thankful for all the people who've prayed for me over the years. I'm thankful for my family, that loves me. I'm thankful for the time God has given me, but I'm ready to see Jesus. I can't wait to see Jesus. Send me home."[1]

The next day, he was gone. Some of his last words were, "There is no downside for me leaving, not in the slightest."[2]

I was, and still am, struck by those words. Even as I type them out, I'm getting teary again.

The day I learned of his death, I wept because he was so ready to go, and I realized I am not.

The intimacy he felt with Jesus was so deep that he longed to be face-to-face with him. Whereas I like my life way too much. And that realization makes me cry.

While I've struggled to embrace many things about my life, I've also had to confront that I don't want eternity more than I want a lot of other things. I think about what I would miss if my life ended tomorrow. I really want to get married one day, to have a family, to see the world, and to continue in my career. And if I'm honest with myself, I want those things more than I want to go to heaven.

Even as we've built lives we love without having everything we want, we are missing one important reality:

This life is not it.

There is a kingdom coming that offers healing to every ache and hole we have in our hearts. But we want the reflections of that kingdom more than we want the realities of it.

Yes, I think God longs for us to experience glimpses and tastes of joy and delight. I believe it's godly and biblical to love the lives he has graciously given us.

But not more than eternity.

I know thinking about death is not usually something we want to do. But understanding the shortness of life makes us live differently. Not because we learn to appreciate what we have more or because we should listen to Tim McGraw and "live like we're dying," but because we have hope in more than this.

There is a kingdom coming that offers healing to every ache and hole we have in our hearts.

All this running after relationships, success, and experiences is not going to fill the holes in our hearts. Once we finally get what we desperately longed for, something else will dissatisfy us. As King Solomon—who had all the riches, relationships, and success a human could have—said, it's "a chasing after the wind" (Ecclesiastes 2:11).

I want more than loving this life.

I think about the 21-year-old version of me. The girl who read a book by Jennie Allen and decided to go all-in with God.[3] The girl who believed God was real and heaven was coming, so she gave up the stereotypical college life. And how much that cost her.

Lately I've been trying to find her again. I know she is somewhere inside. The 30-year-old version of me has seen a lot. Some days I recognize it as maturing, but most days? Most days I wonder if I'm just jaded.

My greatest fear when I was 21 was being normal. I didn't want to chase things in life that didn't really matter. I understood how the reward of following God completely outweighed the risk of not following him.

But life has a way of crowding in. Then risk starts to feel scary, and normal starts to sound really good.

When you've faced some disappointments, the questions start. On certain days, you wonder if God is holding out on you; such as when you know God could intervene, but he doesn't. When what God's Word says and what you see don't match up, it's easy for your soul to become exhausted and your heart to become skeptical.

Maybe longing for steadiness is part of growing up, but I really don't want that to be the case. I don't want my life to be filled with chasing stability and security in the form of a husband, a house, or a new car. I want to get back to the girl who wanted anything but a normal life.

But how?

I want to tell you I've mastered this. That I don't have days when the things I want pale in comparison to life with God. But you already know that would be a lie.

I figure I'm not alone in this. There is a level of feeling behind that will always exist because we are believers.

When your life is no longer lining up with those around you. When you make the hard choice to put away old things and say yes to following God. When you act in obedience even when life is not going the way you want it to. When you continue to follow God regardless of the outcome.

Following Jesus is costly. Sometimes it *does* cost what the world defines as the "good life" or success. It means it'll seem like our friends are moving on without us. It also sometimes means feeling misunderstood and worse, alone.

Often, it makes me feel left out. And to be honest, that's not usually fun. This is the moment when I feel most tempted to throw in the towel and quit. It's just too hard. Too painful.

We like the safety of sameness. But when God calls us as his own and we choose to answer, our lives will look different.

Surrender is the only way. Surrender doesn't always feel safe, but it's actually the most secure way to live.

I rarely think about what I've missed out on because I live in surrender, but I often think about what I would have missed if I didn't.

God isn't after normal, American dream–type lives for us. He is after our hearts. His love for us does not cosign the plans we made for ourselves. But his love for us is so great, he invites us to dream of greater things. Eternal things. Things that will last much longer than feeling behind. In fact, those eternal things will last after our lives on this earth are gone.

Surrender doesn't always feel safe, but it's the most secure way to live.

And even though our lives may end up looking drastically different from anything we could have dreamed, what God has planned for us is so much more satisfying.

For they loved not their lives even unto death (Revelation 12:11).

Our ultimate goal as Christians is not to have a life we love. The goal is to love Jesus and show that love to others.

This is urgent because I'm afraid we are missing it. I'm afraid we're building lives that make us feel better, not lives to build his kingdom. Everything we've done up until this point is good and meaningful work, but if we just stop here, we miss the whole point.

Jesus is coming back. We have races to run, and now that we've addressed the hurdles to running—shame, disappointment, idolatry, and comparison—we can run farther and faster.

We can be who God made us to be. Not for our own sense of glory, but for his.

Because you have a part to play. We talked about it in chapter 9. You, right now, have a role assigned to you by God. He has put you somewhere on purpose. And some of it may have to do with your own sanctification, but a lot of it also has to do with the people around you.

There are people in that job you hate who are lonely and lost.

There are people in your neighborhood who are anxious and afraid.

There are people at your gym who are disappointed and disillusioned with the world.

There are people all around you who are desperate for hope.

And the only hope they have, the only hope we all have, is Jesus. The Son of God. The Savior of the world. The One who died and rose again. And let's not forget this really crucial part: the One who is coming back to make all things new again.

When we are so focused on what we lack or what's ahead, we have to stop and look up.

A few friends have been reading this book as I've written it, and one made an interesting observation: I always seem to be looking up. Whether at popcorn ceilings or the sky. I never noticed it, but she kindly told me she thinks that posture is important. While I may not have thought of it this way, looking up is a solution to not feeling behind.

Looking down at my phone doesn't make me want to get out and live.

Looking sideways—seeing everyone else's jobs, incomes, or relationship statuses—doesn't make me want to use my gifts.

Looking ahead, grasping for better tomorrows, doesn't make me want to show up to my life right now.

Looking up toward God is how we stop feeling behind. There's a better way to live: Even if we don't love our circumstances, and even if we don't have all the things we can pad ourselves with to make us more comfortable, we still love God and look at every day as an opportunity to bring his kingdom here.

Which is so much more satisfying.

When we let go of the standards placed on us by society, we can be free to move forward into the grace God has given us. Life with him is so much better. It's so much better to keep your eyes on eternal things than what's on the internet.

Some of the people around me are trying to live this way. My friends Katie and Jake are considering moving overseas to a country where Christians are not welcome. He has a great job and they have two kids, but they are willing to give up security to tell people about Jesus.

I have friends who are doing this in different ways. One guy I know traded his truck in for a cheaper, less attractive car. Not because he needed to, but because he felt convicted that he had the truck for the wrong reasons and wanted to tear down the idol he had made. The next week, a guy in his Bible study did the same thing.

When we let go of the standards placed on us by society, we can be free to move forward into the grace God has given us.

I could tell you many stories of people I know who are pushing against the stereotypical lifestyle of our city. They are not trying to impress their church friends or become martyrs, but they know God is calling them to a better, more satisfying way of living—a life that isn't driven by status and stuff.

I am not telling you to move overseas or give everything away, but would you be willing to?

Would you believe me if I said you may wind up loving your life a little more if you did?

Some days I want following God to feel easier. For it not to cost me something. But it costs me everything, and that's the point.

This is where I start to get a little preachy.

This book is about helping you realize you are not behind. Do you want to know why that matters? Because we are called to live for God, not for what we want.

Because the enemy wants to distract you from what actually matters.

What matters is not your relationship status.

Or your career success.

Or your material possessions.

Or even the people you call friends.

It's building a kingdom that will outlast *all of that*.

You want to know how to build a life you love without having everything you want? Stop trying to build a life that's all about you, and start building one that's all about Jesus.

That may sound harsh, and maybe to some, extreme. But I'm personally exhausted from the striving. We waste our days chasing the illusion that life, liberty, and the pursuit of happiness are our birthrights, that we are entitled to them. But the reality is, God promises we will "lack nothing" if we fear him (Psalm 34:9). (Yes, I'm quoting Psalm 34 *again*.)

Do we actually believe him?

Living as though you believe you are not behind changes everything!

It's surrendering your ideals, plans, and outcomes to God, who is in control of it all anyway.

It's saying no to what the world says is good and saying yes to what God says is better.

It's giving people around you permission to stop running so hard to catch up.

It's not living in the past wondering if you should have done something differently, but trusting where God has taken and will take you.

It's straight-up acknowledging this world just ain't it.

So often we feel exhausted by the pressure to do and be everything, and look good while doing it.

Believing we're not behind is saying "enough is enough" with that. We can finally catch our breath. Take the weight off our shoulders.

Because it's not all up to you and me.

Dependence on God is the goal. Understanding God is the One in control—not you or me—is the result we are aiming for.

Which feels so backward.

If I trust God is not withholding good things from me, then I am free to enjoy the things in front of me.

Yesterday I wrote in my journal the simplest words to God: "You can have it all again."

And I wrote the same words again today. So, day after day, I'll die to myself a little more and ask the Lord what surrender looks like. Not because it's easy or glamorous or because I think it'll get me what I want. No, because Jesus died for our sins and heaven is real, and life is just too short to worry about everything else.

If I trust God is not withholding good things from me, then I am free to enjoy the things in front of me.

A GOOD GOODBYE

April 2023

I turned out of our neighborhood for the last time last night. I moved into my new, temporary place three weeks ago, but this felt like the final moment I had anticipated having all along.

Madi and I met at the house to do one more sweep of the place before the sale closes this week. I drove there from work on autopilot, as I used to do every day. The last thing I had on my to-do list was take down my curtains. The ones that were slightly uneven. And I thought about the minor meltdown I'd had when I hung them up a few years prior.

I remember trying not to cry while I worked to make them perfectly straight. My skills with a drill weren't ones I desired to sharpen, but I tried anyway. Riley showed up for dinner, walked into my room, and knew instantly that I was not okay. Then she kindly sat with me while I finished the project. Just so I didn't have to be alone.

The crooked curtains symbolized home in a lot of ways. The effort to put them up is not worth it if you don't plan on staying long. I knew it wouldn't be forever, but at the time I was committed to making that place home.

I'd silently bargained with God about never hanging curtains again on my own. I prayed my next move would be the last one.

We went on one last walk with Riley and Victoria and all ended up in tears. As Madi and I walked back to the house, she looked at me and said, "I feel like we grew up here." Which is true. The girls who moved into that house are not the same as the ones who moved out.

On the way home, tears started to fall again. I cried about not having a home, about not knowing what's next, and about feeling behind. But I also felt hopeful because I'm not the same girl who moved into that house.

I didn't have to hang the curtains alone. Riley was there—and while that's not exactly what I was asking God for, I had a friend to sit with me mid-meltdown.

It's the end of a really good season. In some ways it feels like graduating college. And in a lot of ways, I'm tired of that. I want a permanent roommate. I want to stop moving and having to say goodbye.

But this goodbye was good. Because we chose each other, our little neighborhood family. We showed up. And yes, I'm no longer living within walking distance, but my community is still there for me.

I could have just left the curtains behind, but I wanted to take them because they do represent home for me. Now, as I put the folded-up curtains in another box, I don't know where they are going next. I mean, they will go in the storage unit with the rest of my earthly possessions for now, but I'm not sure where they will hang again. Or if I'll hang them with someone else.

But I believe with my whole heart that God knows where they

are going. Just like he knows where I'm going. He has not led me here to abandon me. Just like the day I lay on the sidewalk and saw that rainbow, I am again reminded of his faithfulness. Because as humans we so quickly forget, and I need to be reminded again and again. He provided so much in a season I struggled through.

That house holds good memories—falling in love, first kisses, parties celebrating birthdays, babies, and engagements. I lost count of how many Half Baked Harvest recipes we made in that kitchen and how many times Madi made us rewatch the *Taylor Swift Reputation Stadium Tour* on Netflix.

I know what's ahead will be better than what's behind. Not because I can see it, but because despite the bumps it takes to get there, it usually is. I once thought my best four years happened in college, but then I moved in with Brenna and Shelby. And I never thought it could get better than that. But while each of those chapters held really good things, the next one got even better. I don't always recognize it while it's happening, but I know I'll wake up certain one day I'm living the life I prayed for.

When I let the things I don't have cloud my view of what I do have, I miss so much.

Even this morning I journaled about some things and found myself wanting to focus on unanswered prayers and the things consuming my mind…But then I thought about all God has done. I was letting what I don't know, what I can't see, and what I wish were different steal the joy of what I was living today.

I desperately want to know what's next. I want to know how this book is going to end. I want to know if the relationship I'm in is going to work out. I want to know if I'm even going to stay in this city. And I'm still terrified to get my hopes up about any of it. Because I just don't know how it's going to work out.

Once again, I have a choice. To let the sadness steal my joy, or to hope. I have been temporarily disappointed, but never permanently let down. So the worst that can happen is temporary disappointment.

Because one day, disappointment will end too. One day, all the earthly things I'm so quick to put my hope in will pass away, but I won't care because I'll see Jesus face-to-face. The only One who has always been there, the only One who will satisfy every longing I've ever had. Nothing else will matter.

In the meantime, what a gift to experience life. To know the sadness of saying goodbye because you're saying goodbye to something really good. To hold on to the joyful memories of what has happened. To dream about what could be ahead. To know we can still hope that good is coming.

A couple we are good friends with is moving into the house after us, and they are expecting their first baby. Just like that, life goes on and new chapters are beginning. They get to make their own memories where we have made so many of ours.

This life is not everything. But it is such a gift. May we never forget what a good, good Giver we have.

CHAPTER 13

You Are Not Behind

WE'VE COVERED A lot of ground, friend.

Part of me can't quite believe we made it here. Correction: I can't believe *I* made it here. I knew you could.

In the pages of this book, we've quietly confessed to one another. We've admitted what's hard. We've shared what we really want. We've dared to hope that there's more to life than keeping up or getting ahead.

I have one more confession for you: I really didn't know where we would be at the end of these pages.

I especially didn't know that I'd experience the message of this book so differently while I was writing it than I experienced it when I first pitched it to my editor.

At the time, I thought I'd come to peace with the areas of life that make me feel most behind: my singleness, my living situation, and my job. I believed I'd "gotten the message," which was why I wanted to write this book in the first place. I'd be writing from past experiences and lessons learned. From a healed heart and hopeful future.

That's not what happened.

While the initial chapter outline I wrote before staring the book has mostly remained the same, what ended up in the pages were actual moments of my life being lived in real time. The year I spent writing this book looked so different than I thought it would. And I thought I had a pretty good idea of what it was going to look like! I already had plans written in my calendar.

But then life happened. And you saw how that played out as we journeyed together. Like I said in the introduction, not everything is tied up in a bow. In fact, some bows came completely undone. Meanwhile, new things I never expected entered the picture.

Still, I wanted to share my ups and the downs of wrestling with my behind-ness. Or the moments when I questioned if it *really* was possible to build a life I loved without having everything I wanted. Even though I felt vulnerable letting you see that I might not be a perfect expert at living the message I felt called to share, I hoped you would see yourself in these moments. That you would notice the areas of your life where you were struggling with the same questions, and that you would know you weren't alone.

Maybe that was God's plan from the beginning. To have me live what I am writing to you. While my experiences over the last several years have lent themselves to this book, this message hasn't been nearly as much about my past as it is about what I'm living right now.

It hasn't been the easiest or prettiest year. Even with the help of my editor to polish my stories, the experiences themselves have still been messy.

I'm not on the other side yet, but here in the middle, I can tell God is up to something. Not so much in my external circumstances (although he definitely is working there), but in me. My prayer is that you've opened yourself up to let him do the same in you.

YOU HAVE ALL THE TOOLS YOU NEED

Life is abundant here and now. On the other side of shame from our past and mistakes, we can acknowledge our desires and disappointments and deal with our struggles with idolatry and comparison. There is joy in celebrating along the way. Happiness is a real emotion that our heavenly Father delights in us experiencing (James 1:17).

That's why I want to go back to Hebrews 12, where we started this book:

> Therefore, since we are surrounded by such a great cloud of witnesses, let us throw off everything that hinders and the sin that so easily entangles. And let us run with perseverance the race marked out for us, fixing our eyes on Jesus, the pioneer and perfecter of faith. For the joy set before him he endured the cross, scorning its shame, and sat down at the right hand of the throne of God. Consider him who endured such opposition from sinners, so that you will not grow weary and lose heart (Hebrews 12:1-3).

Now more than ever I wish I could look you in the eye and say these words to you: *Stop believing the lie that you are behind. Because you aren't.*

Like the writer of Hebrews says, we can get easily entangled in sin and hindered by stumbling blocks. And I hope you, like me, are ready to say, "Enough is enough." Let's choose to be done getting sidelined by the enemy and all the extra junk weighing us down.

I want to run the race God has marked out for me. And I want you to run yours too.

Your life is far too beautiful and important to stay stuck in feeling behind.

You are not missing out on potentially bigger and better tomorrows. But you may be missing out on the life God is calling you to today.

I want us both to boldly and bravely *live*.

If you have the Holy Spirit inside of you, then you have every tool you need. The very power that raised Christ from the dead will give you everything you need to thrive in the life God has placed before you (Romans 8:11).

Your decision to live in this power and freedom is so important. Not only so you can personally enjoy your life a little more, but also so you can live each day with confidence and hope—so others can too. When we can get to a place of embracing our present reality, the result will be contagious.

The world is desperate for hope, but you and me? We have hope living in us.

It's not a hope we have to muster up and manipulate (which, Lord knows, I have certainly tried to do). And this hope is not in waiting for everything to turn out a certain way. It's in knowing everything is going to turn out the way God said it would. And that's really good news!

> **When we can get to a place of embracing our present reality, the result will be contagious.**

GOD KEEPS HIS PROMISES

The author of Hebrews tells us about a great cloud of witnesses in chapter 11. He writes about well-known Bible figures including Noah and Abraham, Jacob and Joseph, Moses and David, Sarah and Rahab. The author recaps the highlights of their faith and the victories on the other side of them. But *then*! Then the chapter ends with what can feel like one of the most disappointing verses I've ever read:

These were all commended for their faith, yet *none of them received what had been promised*, since God had planned something better for us so that only together with us would they be made perfect (Hebrews 11:39-40, emphasis added).

I'm sorry, *what?*

As we read Hebrews 11's recollection of tales of the Old Testament, we're likely to miss a crucial part: Though these men and women of faith lived out God's purposes for them, they *still* didn't get to see the things God had promised them come to pass in their lifetime.

God kept *every single promise.* But they did not experience them.

And yet they are held in the highest esteem in all of human history. This passage is known as the "hall of faith" because these men and women believed. They did not quit. They understood God's plan was bigger than just their time.

My biggest prayer is that the same can someday be said of me and you. That we did not quit when life got hard and stopped going our way. Instead, we faced obstacles, dealt with our sin, and threw off every weight and burden that entangled us.

Because don't overlook verse 40: *God had something better planned.*

Today, we've received what they were each promised: Jesus.

Right now, we are living out the promise God made to all those people. And when we experience the heartache of unmet dreams and desires, we can take comfort in remembering that these promises—salvation through Christ, an unending relationship with God, the Holy Spirit within us—are ultimately so much more satisfying than anything else we could want.

So today, what are we waiting for? A dream to come true? A circumstance to change? We don't have to wait for those things to enjoy our days here. We can do that right now.

There's one more promise left: When our time on earth comes to an end, we will be reunited with Jesus. Face-to-face. We will be with him in heavenly glory (Revelation 22:4-5). We can count on that.

In the meantime, we are called to live for him. No more chasing. No more competing. No more getting winded from sprinting to catch up. Instead, we can run with freedom and focus, our eyes on the prize: Jesus himself, awaiting us at the end of the unique race he has laid out for each of us.

Winning our race looks like making it to the end of our days, resting in the fact that we showed up and ran. And that's my vision and prayer: seeing this generation of people running toward the finish line. Regardless of what direction, route, or pace they may be going, they are each focused on winning *their* race.

Friend, you're not behind. Do you believe me yet?

Catching up and getting ahead are overrated anyway. That thing you really want doesn't have the power to fix you. And you're probably never going to finally arrive at a place where you feel perfectly content and at ease in this life. But that's okay; it might even be a good thing. John 16:33 says God promises peace even when we have trouble in this world. That should free us up to love our lives today.

YOU ARE WHERE YOU'RE SUPPOSED TO BE

I still want so many things. Prayers are still unanswered. Desires are still unmet. And I have questions about if or when some dreams will come true.

And yet, I really do love my life.

Because I've fallen back in love with the One who has made it. The One who carries me through each day and invites me to see goodness in the middle of it all.

I've not arrived by any means. I haven't perfectly lived out the message I want you to take away. However, even though my days of longing for more have not disappeared, my days of enjoying life in the meantime have increased.

But I'm more convinced than ever before that God delights in us living in abundance.

So, before we go, I've got some words I don't want you to forget. I want you to say them to yourself on the days you feel behind and tired from trying to keep up. I hope after you put this book on the shelf, you will come back to the next page to remember what is true.

I'm Where
I'm Supposed to Be

Where I am today is the most realistic place I can be. That doesn't make the future dreams I have unrealistic—I'm free to want those dreams to come true. But my happiness and worth don't depend on them happening on my timetable.

Instead of feeling behind, I'm deciding that the experiences of today are helping me get ahead in my preparations for tomorrow. If I embrace today and give it my best where I am, I won't have to worry about missing out on great tomorrows. My goal is to invest my best into today and not get out of breath from grabbing for too much in my tomorrows.

I refuse to chase others.

I refuse to feel like I'm not good enough.

I refuse to feel like I'm losing.

I do not have to manipulate my hope. I do not have to muster up a false sense of contentment or deny what my heart longs for in order to get what I want. Instead, I can put all my hope in the Author of hope, the One who is writing my story.

If I need to grieve what hasn't happened yet, then I will. But at the same time, I will not let grief darken where I'm at. If I would have gotten what I wanted, I would have missed out on what my life is right now.

Life was never meant to give us all the things. We are meant to get some things, enjoy them, and then trust that for today that is what's best. And rest knowing I'm not meant to have the rest right now.

The rest won't fix me.

The rest won't fill me.

The rest won't satisfy me today because it's not meant for today.

Only God has all things at all times. Because only he can carry that. And in his time, he will entrust to me the opportunity to carry other things.

So I will choose to trust that my Father does not withhold good things from me. His goodness is mine in abundance, as long as I choose to look for it.

And while I wait for the rest, I will rest.

Rest in knowing that I have not missed his best.

Rest in knowing that I don't have to catch up.

Rest in knowing that I am not missing out.

Rest in knowing that I don't have to get ahead.

Rest in knowing that I am not behind.

I am right where I am supposed to be: safe, secure, and settled in God's perfect plan for me.

It's your turn now. Go run.

When you trip and fall along the way, it's okay. Get up and keep running. Just don't quit.

I'll be right here, cheering you while you do.

The Next Chapter

OCTOBER 2023

Today, I packed yet another U-Haul filled with my earthly possessions.

I never imagined this day would come as soon as it did. But here I am again. Loading boxes and trying not to cry while I do.

Which is exactly what I said before I moved into the Floyds' basement. That temporary landing spot became the best place for me to be for the sixish months I lived there. It has been an answer to a prayer I didn't even know I prayed.

Part of me is sad to be leaving because it was so nice to be part of someone's family. But that's not what is making me cry. I knew I couldn't stay there forever. Plus, I'm ready to have my own space again.

What's making me cry is that I'm moving to another new city.

Almost four years ago to the day, I moved to Charlotte, North Carolina. I did it because I got a job, and moving seemed like the next right step. I had no idea what my life would look like once I got here. I dreaded leaving home for somewhere so unfamiliar. I had a lot of fear in the face of the unknowns.

But now, I don't want to leave.

It's kind of crazy thinking about how fast it's all happening, and yet I find myself asking the same questions I showed up here with:

Will starting over be hard?
What will life look like?
Will I make new friends?
Will my current friends move on without me?
Am I missing out?
How long will it take to "catch back up"?
I feel behind all over again.

Though the next chapter of life promises a lot of really good things, this chapter has been really hard to let go of.

I showed up in Charlotte without knowing a soul, and now I'm crying again because the people here have become my family. And imagining day-to-day life without them makes me sad.

So much has changed in four years.

Even since we started this journey together, I've gone through multiple roommates and homes. If you're counting, that's a grand total of 22 different roommates in 12 years. Bless it.

I've wondered where God is in the midst of it all. And I had no idea this part would be added to our last few pages together.

But here we are. It happened. While I feel pretty blind to what's ahead, the future is happening whether I'm ready or not.

I still can't believe I did all of this.

I built a life I really loved, well before I'd had everything I wanted. All the ideas we talked about in this book—getting honest about my reality, grieving, wanting, tearing down idols in my heart, letting go of comparing myself—they worked. I experienced them firsthand.

Our conversations have shown me so much of who God is, and my life has been abundantly full this year, even in the hard moments.

Which makes it so much harder to leave the city I've come to call home.

As I'm writing, the ring on my left hand keeps catches the light, and whenever it does, it shines. And I can't help but smile.

I'm still getting used to wearing it. And every single day, I find myself more in love with the man who gave it to me.

An engagement doesn't feel totally real yet. This came out of nowhere—the most unexpected gift, at the most unexpected time. I went into writing a book about being behind, thinking I would spend these years single. No, really; I even told people I thought God would keep me in this place because I needed to truly experience feeling behind in this area.

How wrong I was.

I never imagined there would be a last name printed on the cover of this book that was different than the one I had when I signed my contract.

Part of me is asking, *Why?*

Why me?

Why right now?

To be honest, I don't really know why it's happening now. I've wanted this for so long, but I don't know why God decided this was the right timing.

This change—starting a relationship, falling in love, getting engaged—didn't happen because I finally found the perfect balance between wanting something and not wanting it too much. It wasn't because I prayed enough or finally cracked the code of contentment.

It wasn't even because I managed to stop manipulating my hopes. You've read the whole story; you know how much I struggled to do that. Even today I am wrestling with how to not temper my excitement and expectations for what's ahead. Because part of me is still scared of disappointment.

I don't think the timing had anything to do with me at all, actually. God, in *his* timing, just knew. And I might be the most surprised it's happening right now.

Despite the love and joy and gratitude I feel, those emotions haven't taken away my fear of being behind as I move to a new place and start over again.

And I'm wondering if that may be the point of this.

We can always find reasons to feel we are behind—not because we are truly short of the line, but because the line is constantly moving.

Once we arrive at one destination, another one waits ahead. We will never stop moving forward, even if we try to stand still.

So we have to trust we are where God wants us to be.

As I load the last boxes into the truck, I look up at the sky. This time I don't see a rainbow reminding me of God's promises. The October leaves are bright with color and starting to fall. Which is as poetic as it feels. A new season is beginning.

As tears roll down my face, I take a deep breath and whisper, "Thank you, Lord."

I know what's ahead has good in it because God has already gone before me. He is not leading me somewhere he has not already been.

He has been faithful every step of the way. Not once did he leave me. Even when I could not see him or feel him or hear him, he was here.

I'm a different girl from the one who showed up to this city four years ago. A little more weathered, with more creases in my face to prove it. I know God in a way I didn't before.

If I've learned anything, it's that I really can stand on my own two feet with God. Regardless of my relationship status, geographical location, the amount of money in my bank account, my career success or failure, the friends I make, or anything the world tries to sell me, all I need is him.

I'm leaving with more trust in God. He was and is the most faithful friend to me.

After we close the truck, Lucas takes my hand and pulls me

into a hug. I try not to get my tears and snot all over his shirt. But he lets me cry and holds me a minute longer.

As we drive away, I cry some more, but I also pray. Thanking God for every single detail of a chapter of my life that has been so much better than one I ever could have written for myself. Every time I doubted, he came through.

I have no idea what's next. Or how hard it may be.

But I know one thing:

I am not behind. Or caught up. Or ahead.

Neither are you.

The Author of our stories has given us precious time to love and to live. We just have to choose to embrace it.

But remember, the small ache for more that doesn't seem to go away is a good thing. It's the reminder that we all need the abundant, eternal life promised to those of us who are in Christ. And that life is on the other side of this one.

Right now, we can trust him with the details. He has not once stopped being in control, and he never will.

I take one last look in the rearview mirror and silently picture myself closing the chapter of a really good book.

Big inhale. Slow exhale.

The story was never about me, but I am eager to see what he writes next.

How to Know
Jesus Personally

THESE ARE THE most important pages of this book, because the words we exchange here are the ones that will matter for eternity.

Regardless of what you've heard or experienced about God, this is true:

God is real. He loves you (John 3:16).

God created the world and everything in it. He designed it all to be good, and humans walked in perfect fellowship with him (Genesis 1:31). But then the first two humans disobeyed God by doing the one thing he'd asked them not to do. Because of that, sin entered the world. Sin has separated us from God ever since, and sin leads to death (Romans 3:23; 6:23).

But God did not just leave us there. He had a plan to wipe away sin so he could have a relationship with us. He sent his only Son, who was both perfectly God and perfectly human, to live a life without sin and then die a martyr's death he did not deserve—a death that covered our sin (Romans 5:8).

His name was Jesus.

The good news is that Jesus rose from the dead, and the Bible says when we confess with our mouths and believe in our hearts that Jesus is our Lord, we are saved from the death of sin (John 1:12).

So if you believe in your heart that this is true, here are some words to confess with your mouth:

> *God, I need you. I know that without you, I cannot save myself from the grip and weight of my sin. I believe you sent Jesus, your Son, to save me. I believe he lived the life I cannot live so I could come before you freely. I confess Jesus is my Savior and Lord. Help me live for you. Thank you for how much you love me. Change my heart. Change my life. In Jesus's name, amen.*

If you prayed this, I highly recommend finding a local church to talk with you more about what it looks like to follow Jesus. If you need help finding one, you can send me a message on social media, and I'd love to help you. You can also search your location on www.TheGospelCoalition.org/churches to discover a list of churches near you.

"What Do I Really Want?" Chart

IDENTIFY THE KEY THINGS YOU WANT THAT YOU DON'T
HAVE CONTROL OVER YET:

WHY DO YOU WANT EACH OF THOSE THINGS?

HOW CAN YOU TAKE THE REASONS YOU WANT THOSE
THINGS AND APPLY THEM TO YOUR LIFE IN AN
UNEXPECTED WAY?

IDENTIFY THE KEY THINGS YOU WANT THAT YOU DON'T HAVE CONTROL OVER YET:

WHY DO YOU WANT EACH OF THOSE THINGS?

HOW CAN YOU TAKE THE REASONS YOU WANT THOSE THINGS AND APPLY THEM TO YOUR LIFE IN AN UNEXPECTED WAY?

IDENTIFY THE KEY THINGS YOU WANT THAT YOU DON'T
HAVE CONTROL OVER YET:

WHY DO YOU WANT EACH OF THOSE THINGS?

HOW CAN YOU TAKE THE REASONS YOU WANT THOSE
THINGS AND APPLY THEM TO YOUR LIFE IN AN
UNEXPECTED WAY?

Additional Resources on Spiritual Disciplines

HERE ARE SOME definitions and additional resources for practicing spiritual disciplines in your life.

GLOSSARY

Fasting and feasting: abstaining from food in order to seek God and celebrating with food in community.

Prayer: talking to God about anything and everything.

Reading the Bible: reading, studying, and understanding the living and active words of God that he gave us.

Sabbath: taking a day off work to rest, delight, and worship.

Silence and solitude: taking time away from people and noise and making space to recharge and listen to God.

ADDITIONAL BOOKS AND RESOURCES

The Ruthless Elimination of Hurry by John Mark Comer

Praying Like Monks, Living Like Fools by Tyler Staton

Rest for Your Soul by Wendy Blight

Beautiful Resistance: The Joy of Conviction in a Culture of Compromise by Jon Tyson

Liturgy of the Ordinary: Sacred Practices in Everyday Life by Tish Harrison Warren

Rule of Life podcast series by Practicing the Way

30 Questions
to Ask Your Friend at Coffee
Instead of Asking "What's New?"

I RECOMMEND TAKING a picture of these pages and saving them to your phone so you'll have them when you need them.

1. What's something you've learned lately?
2. Have you read any good books, listened to any good podcasts, or watched any good shows?
3. What is something you've enjoyed doing with friends lately?
4. Is there something that's been heavy on your mind?
5. What's one thing you are looking forward to this week?
6. What was the best part of your day yesterday?
7. What are you dreaming about?
8. Who is a voice you are thankful for in your life right now?
9. How can I be a better friend to you?
10. What's something you need but are afraid to ask for?
11. What do you think motivates you?
12. What was the last thing you were influenced to buy?
13. What is the hardest thing going on in your world lately?

14. What's something you've been wanting to do that we could do together?

15. How is God speaking to you?

16. What was the last good meal you had?

17. What's causing you stress?

18. How can I pray for you?

19. What or who is bringing you joy right now?

20. Is there anything you want to talk about today?

21. If money was no object and you could do any job in the world, what would it be and why?

22. What do you wish your friends understood about you?

23. What is making you feel like you are behind right now?

24. What is something you know is a lie but feels true?

25. In what area of your life are you struggling to trust God today?

26. What is something you are waiting for?

27. Are there any routines in your life that are really helpful these days?

28. What feels challenging right now?

29. Have you tried any good restaurants or coffee shops you'd recommend?

30. What's something you're obsessed with?

Notes

CHAPTER 2: I FEEL LIKE I'M MISSING OUT...BECAUSE I KIND OF

1. "The COVID-19 Economy's Effects on Food, Housing, and Employment Hardships," Center on Budget and Policy Priorities, last modified February 10, 2022, https://www.cbpp.org/research/poverty-and-inequality/tracking-the-covid-19-recessions-effects-on-food-housing-and.

2. Ibid.

3. Tovia Smith, "Welcome to the wedding boom. How couples are handling the busiest season in 40 years," National Public Radio, March 24, 2022, https://www.npr.org/2022/03/24/1088053579/wedding-boom-couples-handling-busiest-season-40-years.

4. Anna Brown, "Most Americans who are 'single and looking' say dating has been harder during the pandemic," Pew Research Center, April 6, 2022, https://www.pewresearch.org/short-reads/2022/04/06/most-americans-who-are-single-and-looking-say-dating-has-been-harder-during-the-pandemic.

5. John Gramlich, "Mental health and the pandemic: What U.S. surveys have found," Pew Research Center, March 2, 2023, https://www.pewresearch.org/short-reads/2023/03/02/mental-health-and-the-pandemic-what-u-s-surveys-have-found.

CHAPTER 3: WAIT, I'M NOT THE ONLY ONE?

1. Sandee LaMotte, "The pandemic may have created a nation of problem drinkers—and many are women," *CNN.com*, last modified January 25, 2022, https://www.cnn.com/2022/01/22/ealth/pandemic-drinking-problem-wellness/index.html.

2. Tracy Hampton, "Study hold warning on pandemic drinking," *Harvard Gazette*, January 4, 2022, https://news.harvard.edu/gazette/story/2022/01/covid-related-drinking-linked-to-rise-in-liver-disease.

3. Richa Agarwal et al., "Effect of increased screen time on eyes during COVID-19 pandemic," *Journal of Family Medicine and Primary Care* 11, no. 7 (July 2022): 3643, https://journals.lww.com/jfmpc/Fulltext/2022/07000/Effect_of_increased_screen_time_on_eyes_during.40.aspx.

4. Fabio Zattoni, Murat Gul, "The Impact of COVID-19 Pandemic on Pornography Habits: A Global Analysis of Google Trends," (November 28, 2020), https://www.nature.com/articles/s41443-020-00380-w.

5. Kupcova, I., Danisovic, L., Klein, M., & Harsanyi, S., "Effects of the COVID-19

pandemic on mental health, anxiety, and depression" (2023), https://www.ncbi.nlm.nih.gov/pmc/articles/PMC10088605.

6. C.S. Lewis, *Mere Christianity* (New York: HarperOne, 1980), 137.

CHAPTER 4: IS THIS MY PUNISHMENT?

1. Page Brooks and D. A. Neal, "Theodicy," ed. John D. Barry et al., *The Lexham Bible Dictionary* (Bellingham, WA: Lexham Press, 2016).

2. *Anything: The Prayer that Unlocked My God and My Soul* by Jennie Allen totally changed my life my junior year of college. Maybe this book would change yours too.

CHAPTER 5: YOU MIGHT ALWAYS GRIEVE WHAT DID (OR DID NOT) HAPPEN

1. Lysa TerKeurst, *Good Boundaries and Goodbyes: Loving Others without Losing the Best of Who You Are* (Nashville: Nelson Books, 2022), 202.

2. https://www.shiva.com/learning-center/sitting-shiva.

3. Adam Young, "138 How To Heal from Sorrow and Grief Part 5 with Mary Ellen Owen," May 1, 2023, in *The Place We Find Ourselves*, podcast, https://open.spotify.com/episode/6TyGjOxM9rsCczXryYbHAr?si=wTJynp5TTD6ADV0UCsINYQ.

4 Adam Young, "123 Is Hope Reasonable?" October 24, 2022, in *The Place We Find Ourselves*, podcast, https://open.spotify.com/episode/2sfeeXBmkZK99YGlVSnhVx.

CHAPTER 6: WHAT DO I *REALLY* WANT?

1. Millennial life: "How young adulthood today compares with prior generations," Pew Research Center, February 14, 2019, https://www.pewresearch.org/social-trends/2019/02/14/millennial-life-how-young-adulthood-today-compares-with-prior-generations-2.

CHAPTER 7: DO I WANT THIS TOO MUCH?

1. Timothy Keller, *Counterfeit Gods: The Empty Promises of Money, Sex, and Power, and the Only Hope that Matters* (New York: Penguin, 2009), 3.

CHAPTER 8: THEY ARE NOT AHEAD

1. Julia Kagan, "Lifestyle Creep: What It Is, How It Works," Investopedia, November 29, 2020, https://www.investopedia.com/terms/l/lifestyle-creep.asp.

2. Kirsten Weir, "Nurtured by Nature," *Monitor on Psychology* 51, no. 3 (April 1, 2020): https://www.apa.org/monitor/2020/04/nurtured-nature.

CHAPTER 10: AN OBVIOUS (BUT UNLIKELY) WAY TO LOVE YOUR LIFE

1. *Baker's Evangelical Dictionary of Biblical Theology*, s.v. "Celebrate, Celebration," by William J. Woodruff, Bible Study Tools, accessed December 6, 2023, https://www.chicagomanualofstyle.org/book/ed17/part3/ch14/psec233.html.

CHAPTER II: WHEN THE THING YOU LOOKED FORWARD TO THE MOST MADE YOU FEEL THE WORST ABOUT YOURSELF

1 Lysa TerKeurst, *Unglued: Making Wise Choices in the Midst of Raw Emotions* (Grand Rapids: Zondervan, 2012), 72.

CHAPTER 12: THIS ISN'T WHAT IT'S ALL ABOUT

1. Tim Keller (@timkellernyc), "Health Update: Today, Dad is being discharged from the hospital to receive hospice care at home. Over the past few days, he has asked us to pray with him often," Instagram, May 18, 2023, https://www.instagram.com/p/CsZoqtRRvhg.

2. Tim Keller (@timkellernyc), "Timothy J. Keller, husband, father, grandfather, mentor, friend, pastor, and scholar died this morning at home. Dad waited until he was alone with Mom," Instagram, May 19, 2023, https://www.instagram.com/p/CsboBfrg-ps.

3. Yes, I referenced *Anything* by Jennie Allen twice in this book, but it's that good.

Acknowledgements

FUN FACT: This is always the first page I read when I start a new book.

I love getting to see who helped shape the author and how their fingerprints touch each page. Thinking about the people on this page and ones not mentioned brings tears of gratitude to my eyes and reminds me of the Lord's extreme kindness to me.

Mom and Dad—for introducing me to Jesus. I will tell people till the day I die that I hit the jackpot in the parent lottery. Every prayer you prayed and sacrifice you made for us is something I wish I could attempt to repay in my lifetime. I love you both.

Patrick, Abby, and Micah—my day ones. Sidekicks. Teammates. Best friends. I loved growing up with you. Being adults together may be my new favorite part. I am a better person because of you.

Riley (and Will), Elizabeth (and Grant), Katie (and Jake), Victoria (and Brandon), Sarah (and Walker), Anna Lee, Katie (and JH)—you are the best friends a girl could ask for. Thank you for loving me, feeding me, praying with me and for me, and for not letting me quit or leave Charlotte when I wanted to. I love you all so much.

Brenna and Shelby—for living this with me. Long live the Bae House.

Lysa—I still pinch myself that I get to learn from you, but more than that, it is an honor to be your friend. Thank you for faithfulness and selflessly giving of yourself so more people can experience the fullness of Jesus. I know heaven will be more crowded because of you.

Meredith and the entire Proverbs 31 Ministries team—I love you all. I love what we get to do. Thank you for championing me in every area of life, especially this book. Madi and Shae—my content junkies, you carried me from start to finish.

Wendy—you have been the greatest mentor and prayer warrior through all of this. Thank you.

Randi, Caroline, and Kelsey—this book started on the beach in Cape Cod. Shelby and Shelby, for always cheering me on. Paying for friends in college was well worth the return on investment. Can't wait for our next reunion!

Scott, Chris, Ryan, Wade, and the 2015 Cru team—first off, I'm sorry on behalf of the 22-year-old version of me. But thank you for graciously handing me the microphone and telling me I wasn't too messed up to work in ministry. Your patience, friendship, and leadership has shaped so much of who I am today.

Citizens Church, my CG, and Tim—I love church and Jesus more because of you.

Harry and Allyson—for opening your home and inviting me into your family. So many of these pages were written on the prayer porch, and so much celebrating happened on the party porch. I pray you reap a hundredfold harvest for what you've sown into me.

Tom and Jane—for speaking life into my future and pastoring me for decades. You have pioneered my life of faith, and I am forever grateful.

Lisa and Jerry, Grandma and Ken—your love and generosity over the years made it possible for this to happen. Thank you, times a million!

The Harvest House team and Emma—you fought for a message from a first-time author with hardly a platform, and I am so grateful you took a chance on me. Working with you has been a dream!

Lucas, my best friend and teammate for life—you were the most surprising ending to this chapter. I cannot wait to write the next one, together.

Jesus, words fall short. I still can't believe this is the story you've written for my life. I wouldn't change a second of it. Your love is better than life, and I hope all my days reflect that.

ABOUT THE AUTHOR

MEGHAN RYAN ASBURY is an author and speaker who loves to hype people up to pursue Jesus so they don't miss the best part of life. After graduating from the University of Florida with a bachelor's in English, she worked for several years in college ministry as part of Cru and other international organizations. She has also coauthored two Bible studies, *Ruth* and *Praying Through the Psalms* with Proverbs 31 Ministries. She's determined not to let her generation waste their lives trying to be comfortable, but instead find their callings and run after them. When she's not surrounded by friends, you can usually find her reading a book or doing something outdoors. A Florida beach girl born and raised, she and her husband currently live in Nashville, Tennessee. You can connect with her at AlwaysMeghan.com and on Instagram @MeghanRyanAsbury.

To learn more about Harvest House books and
to read sample chapters, visit our website:

www.HarvestHousePublishers.com

HARVEST HOUSE PUBLISHERS
EUGENE, OREGON